The Rise of AI-Powered Companies

Inspiring the Next Game: Strategy Ideas for Forward Looking Leaders

BCG Henderson Institute

The Rise of AI-Powered Companies

Edited by
François Candelon and Martin Reeves

DE GRUYTER

ISBN 978-3-11-077509-9
e-ISBN (PDF) 978-3-11-077511-2
e-ISBN (EPUB) 978-3-11-077519-8
ISSN 2701-8857

Library of Congress Control Number: 2022940841

Bibliographic information published by the Deutsche Nationalbibliothek
The Deutsche Nationalbibliothek lists this publication in the Deutsche Nationalbibliografie;
detailed bibliographic data are available on the internet at http://dnb.dnb.de.

© 2022 The BCG Henderson Institute
Cover image: sesame/DigitalVision Vectors/Getty Images
Typesetting: Integra Software Services Pvt. Ltd.
Printing and binding: CPI books GmbH, Leck

www.degruyter.com

Acknowledgments

We would like to acknowledge all of the authors whose work appears on the following pages: Elias Baltassis, François Candelon, Cathy Carlisi, Rodolphe Charme di Carlo, Michael Chu, Midas De Bondt, Bowen Ding, Sylvain Duranton, Hind El Bedraoui, Theodoros Evgeniou, Tian Feng, Andrea Gallego, Matthieu Gombeaud, Su Min Ha, Shervin Khodabandeh, David Kiron, Burt LaFountain, Karen Lellouche Tordjman, Daniel Lim, Colleen McDonald, Steven D. Mills, Sam Ransbotham, Tom Reichert, Massimo Russo, Maximiliano Santinelli, Georgie Stokol.

We would also like to acknowledge the broader BCG Henderson Institute community: our Fellows, Ambassadors, and operations teams over the year, who have all made invaluable contributions to our research; our academic collaborators, who have expanded our horizons of new ideas; and our BCG practice area partners, who have collaborated with us on several of these articles.

https://doi.org/10.1515/9783110775112-202

About the BCG Henderson Institute

The BCG Henderson Institute is the Boston Consulting Group's think tank, dedicated to exploring and developing valuable new insights from business, technology, economics, and science by embracing the powerful technology of ideas. The Institute engages leaders in provocative discussion and experimentation to expand the boundaries of business theory and practice, and to translate innovative ideas from within and beyond business.

https://doi.org/10.1515/9783110775112-203

Contents

Part I: **The AI-Powered Company**

Part II: **The Path to Becoming AI-Powered**

Section A: **Data Strategy**

Section B: **Human-AI Collaboration**

Section C: **Responsible AI and the Social License to Operate**

Introduction

We stand at a landmark turning point. A turning point that is the new Industrial Revolution; a complete game-change in the business landscape of all sectors; the global rise in the quality of life and a more sustainable way of living. The turning point is *artificial intelligence*.

With the ability to process massive amounts of data instantaneously even at extremely granular levels, while continuously improving and learning by itself, AI is whizzing us into the next future. Hyper-personalization and automation are just the beginning. In another decade or two, autonomous cars may be the norm and instant translation could render language differences obsolete. Companies may be predicting demand and supply to a T, radically reducing costs, waste, and uncertainties. The velocity of innovation will grow exponentially, as we have already seen with the development of the mRNA vaccine for COVID-19 where AI played a critical role in finding the optimal sequence design. This powerful technology also brings risks – as is the case with most technological breakthroughs – but if carefully managed, AI is set to change our lives for the better, very quickly.

The business landscape is gearing up for a generational change to AI-powered companies. Take ByteDance, the parent company of the wildly popular TikTok. Founded only nine years ago with AI at the heart of its numerous app products, the company is on track to become one of the most valuable businesses in the world with an estimated valuation of $370 billion according to Bloomberg. The smartest traditional companies are also sensing the change and morphing into AI-powered businesses. Rio Tinto is investing $2.6 billion to build an "intelligent mine" with autonomous trucks, trains, and even drills that will optimize production, reduce waste, and allow remote operation for enhanced safety. Energy giant Repsol's ambitious digital transformation features AI at its core – taking up 70% of the 280 initiatives along the entire value chain – to optimize operations and reach net zero emissions by 2050. Our 2020 global study of more than 3,000 executives on AI adoption revealed that six out of ten organizations are piloting or deploying AI solutions.

The AI-powered companies will not only lead, but become the norm in the next decade. This book examines some of the most successful examples of AI-powered companies in Part I and what it takes to become one in Part II. Chapters 1 to 3 demonstrate how AI-enabled countries across the globe – from the US to China – stayed resilient and strong in face of COVID-19, and how they will continue to stay resilient in the future. Chapter 4 delves into how AI is increasingly driving revenue through activities such as product development, beyond the more common use cases of automation and cost savings. Chapter 5 examines how AI is transforming the B2C business with unprecedented amounts of consumer data

https://doi.org/10.1515/9783110775112-205

and new channels. Chapter 6 glimpses into the future by exploring how some businesses may become completely autonomous with AI.

Part II of the book is divided into three key elements that, based on our experience and research, are critical enablers to becoming AI-powered. The first element is a solid data strategy, so Chapter 7 starts with the importance of data alchemy: using continuously refreshed and broadly gathered data to draw actionable conclusions. Chapters 8 to 10 dive into new forms of data sharing and how companies should think about governance and privacy risks.

The second key element that makes a successful AI-powered company is establishing the ideal human-AI collaboration. Chapter 11 lays out the key results of the 2020 AI Global Executive Study with MIT *Sloan Management Review*, examining the various human-AI interactions deployed by leading AI adopters – from AI as automator to AI as illuminator – and mutual learning installed between humans and AI. Chapter 12 summarizes the key findings from the 2021 version of the same report, demonstrating how AI helps build a stronger team culture including better collaboration and team morale. In Chapter 13, we examine the concept of "human + AI productivity," a new perspective on productivity to bring optimal synergy between the two agents.

The third element to becoming AI-powered is "responsible AI and the social license" to operate. For successful adoption of AI solutions, both internally with employees and externally with customers, businesses must create a social license for AI to operate to increase acceptability (Chapter 14). Finally, in Chapters 15 to 17, we delve into the importance of "responsible AI," and the critical steps needed to ensure this is integrated into the decision-making process and subsequent actions.

We hope that this book helps guide organizations in making the critical leap to become AI-powered – the only way to lead, or at least survive, the coming decade.

Part I: **The AI-Powered Company**

François Candelon, Tom Reichert, Sylvain Duranton,
Rodolphe Charme di Carlo, Midas De Bondt

Chapter 1
The Rise of the AI-Powered Company in the Post-Crisis World

For some companies, global shocks have historically brought moments of truth. They can rapidly alter the business landscape and the terms of competition, often in ways that aren't immediately apparent. But companies that make bold moves during challenging times can turn adversity into advantage.[1] The SARS outbreak of 2003 is often credited with giving rise to e-commerce giants such as Alibaba and JD.com, for example, while companies such as American Express and Starbucks pivoted during the global financial crisis of 2008–2009 to digital operating models that enabled them to thrive and dramatically increase shareholder value.

In this sense, COVID-19 is likely to be no different from other crises. It will greatly accelerate several major trends that were already well underway before the outbreak and that will continue as companies shift their focus to recovery. For instance, rather than heavily concentrating sourcing and production in a few low-cost locations, companies will build more redundancy into their value chains. Consumers will purchase more and more goods and services online. And increasing numbers of people will work remotely.

We believe that the application of artificial intelligence will be immensely valuable in helping companies adapt to these trends. Advanced robots that can recognize objects and handle tasks that previously required humans will promote the operation of factories and other facilities 24/7, in more locations and with little added cost. AI-enabled platforms will help companies better simulate live work environments and create on-demand labor forces. Through machine learning and advanced data analytics, AI will help companies detect new consumption patterns and deliver "hyperpersonalized" products to online customers. The most successful use cases will be those that seamlessly combine AI with human judgment and experience.

Some companies that are on the forefront of these trends and have already begun the AI journey will thrive in the post-COVID world. Again, history provides

---

1 https://www.bcg.com/publications/2020/covid-19-reaction-rebound-recession-reimagination.

https://doi.org/10.1515/9783110775112-001

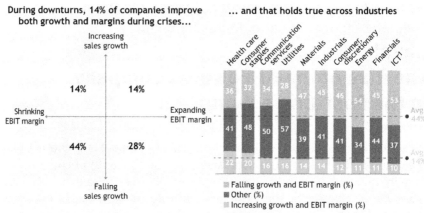

During downturns, 14% of companies improve both growth and margins during crises...

... and that holds true across industries

Sources: S&P Compustat and Capital IQ; BCG Henderson Institute.
[1] Information and communications technology.

Figure 1.1: Across industries, some companies thrive during crises.

a guide: during the four previous global economic downturns, 14% of companies were actually able to *increase* both sales growth and profit margins, according to Boston Consulting Group research (Figure 1.1). The majority of companies, however, are at the very early stages of the journey – or have yet to begin.

Success will not be easy. Some companies have already launched AI use cases that will be helpful in the current crisis. The challenge will be to scale them up. Those that do will be better able to navigate uncertain supply and demand, adjust to disruptions in operations and supply chains, allocate their workforces, and adapt to sharp changes in consumer confidence and priorities.

Digital natives may have an initial edge. Other companies will have to act quickly to acquire the skills, capabilities, and ways of working needed to begin the AI journey. But regardless of their starting point, companies must look beyond the COVID-19 crisis and begin focusing on transformations that put AI at their core.

Why AI Will Be a Must in the Post-Covid World

Most companies already have extensive experience with digital applications such as automation and basic data analytics. But AI, which enables machines to solve problems and take actions that in the past could only be done by humans, goes far beyond that. AI tools analyze immense volumes of data to learn underlying patterns, thus enabling computer systems to make complex decisions, predict human behavior, and recognize images and human speech, among many other things. AI-enabled systems also continuously learn and adapt.

These capabilities will be enormously valuable as companies confront and adapt to the new reality of the current crisis and its aftermath (Figure 1.2).

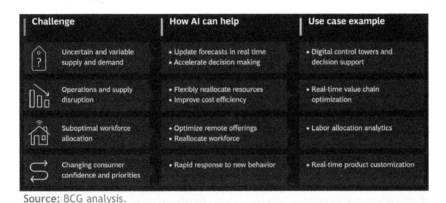

Challenge	How AI can help	Use case example
Uncertain and variable supply and demand	• Update forecasts in real time • Accelerate decision making	• Digital control towers and decision support
Operations and supply disruption	• Flexibly reallocate resources • Improve cost efficiency	• Real-time value chain optimization
Suboptimal workforce allocation	• Optimize remote offerings • Reallocate workforce	• Labor allocation analytics
Changing consumer confidence and priorities	• Rapid response to new behavior	• Real-time product customization

Source: BCG analysis.

Figure 1.2: How AI Can Support Companies.

This new reality will significantly impact companies' costs, revenues, and operating models. Below we assess how the global business landscape is changing along three dimensions – value chain redundancy, shifting consumption patterns, and remote ways of working – and the role that AI can play in enabling companies to thrive and seize competitive advantage in this new environment (Figure 1.3).

Value Chain Redundancy

Not long ago, optimizing costs and time was the overarching objective in the design of global manufacturing footprints, supply chains, and logistical support. Often, that meant concentrating production in high-volume factories in one or two low-cost nations. Inventory and excess capacity were equated with waste. But recently, rising economic nationalism and trade barriers (two aspects of the "new globalization") began forcing companies to rethink their supply chain strategies and rediscover the merits of redundancy. The COVID-19 crisis, which has disrupted global supply chains, has moved redundancy higher

New reality	How AI can help
• Uncertainty requires redundancy, which inevitably means increased costs	• AI enables the greater scale and scope needed to build redundancy while minimizing cost
• Consumption patterns are moving toward e-commerce and other digital models • Consumers may increasingly distinguish essential from luxury items	• AI optimizes detection of new consumption patterns and allows for hyperpersonalization • AI can improve R&D, innovation, and new-product development
• Remote ways of working are becoming the new normal • On-demand labor is becoming more important	• AI-based companies are equipped for new ways of working • AI enables on-demand labor through more precise sales and supplier predictions

Source: BCG analysis.

Figure 1.3: The COVID-19 crisis is accelerating the shift to a new reality.

up on companies' agendas as a means of reducing risk and weathering the next global shock.

But redundancy and duplication entail significant cost. AI offers the potential for companies to build resilience into manufacturing operations and supply chains, while at the same time minimizing costs and damage to margins. AI enables manufacturers to optimize costs in each factory through predictive maintenance and better planning. It also allows them to operate a larger number of small, efficient facilities nearer to customers – rather than a few massive factories in low-wage nations – by deploying advanced manufacturing technologies such as 3D printing and autonomous robots that require few workers.

A leading shoe manufacturer, for example, illustrates AI's potential to boost scale at minimal additional cost. The company now assembles some of its shoes 20 times faster using advanced robots that can recognize, pick up, and stack a wide variety of materials – tasks that were previously done by humans. What's more, factories of the future will increasingly be able to operate around the clock, reducing the risk of closure forced by health crises.

Changing Consumption Patterns

The pandemic is already drastically altering consumption habits worldwide – and affecting companies' revenues – as people make more purchases online and consume food and beverages exclusively at home. Amazon is dramatically ramping up its fulfillment capacity, while online grocery marketplaces in China are reporting huge increases in deliveries of fresh vegetables. Movies are being released for digital streaming without even being released in theaters, and fitness companies such as Peloton and Hydrow are launching digital home-fitness services. What's more, long periods of forced isolation, combined with anxiety about an economic recession, could cause consumers to cut back on luxury items in favor of essentials.

As their focus shifts to recovery, more companies are likely to deploy AI-enabled solutions to reignite topline growth. Thanks to its ability to analyze data from myriad sources, AI has unparalleled potential to discover emerging trends and identify changes in consumer preferences. Even in a human-centered industry like fashion, some companies are augmenting their business intelligence capabilities with AI to amplify weak signals and detect trends early on, such as which colors are likely to be popular in the coming season. AI also enables companies to hyperpersonalize products in order to improve customer engagement and sales. Starbucks' Deep Brew platform, for example, makes coffee suggestions based on the weather, the time of day, or a customer's previous purchases and taste profile.

AI can also enhance the ideation process involved in creating new product offerings, and it can significantly accelerate research and development in industries such as pharmaceuticals, which has traditionally relied on a lengthy trial-and-error process to develop new drugs. Makers of fast-moving consumer goods are analyzing the gold mine of consumer data on Alibaba's TMIC consumer analytics platform to develop new products tailored to Chinese consumers (such as a chili-flavored Snickers® candy bar) and to monitor the performance of new products. Finally, AI-enabled generative design can autonomously identify an optimal product design from a set of system requirements in the development of everything from buildings and chairs to aircraft components.

Remote Ways of Working

Some of the massive shift to remote work due to the pandemic may be temporary. But much of it will persist as more people experience the benefits of avoiding hour-long commutes, and more managers find they can work effectively from home. The flexible working arrangements and on-demand labor models associated with the so-called the "New Freelancers"[2] will become more common.

---

2 https://www.bcg.com/publications/2019/new-freelancers-tapping-talent-gig-economy.

Companies will need to leverage innovative ways of engaging human resources to mitigate the risk of further disruptions and remain competitive. AI is no silver bullet for implementing new ways of working, but it can play an important role. To begin with, AI-powered companies have natural advantages in remote work situations because they tend to be built around modularity and agility, which are prerequisites to success in software-centric businesses. AI also supports online marketplaces for high-skilled, on-demand labor. Upwork, for instance, is an AI-enabled platform that connects freelance professionals with potential employers, while Google's Kaggle allows an online community of data scientists and machine-learning practitioners to collaborate and solve data challenges. Finally, AI tools enable companies to use predictive analytics to more precisely forecast sales and operational challenges, such as labor needs and supply disruptions.

Putting AI at the Core of Business and Operating Models

The current crisis and its aftermath should motivate companies to adjust their business models to the new reality. Winners will reinvent themselves by putting software, data, and AI at the core of their organizations. Digitally native companies can serve as inspiration. AI is already at the heart of some leading ride-hailing platforms, for example, identifying the best routes, onboarding drivers, and even helping to detect fraud. Some long-established incumbents in sectors as diverse as mass retail and consumer finance are now transforming themselves in preparation for an AI-based future.

Such a transformation requires that AI be regarded as central to the business model that differentiates a company and defines how it creates value, as well as to its operating model – the systems, processes, and capabilities that deliver value. Data must underlie every aspect of the operating model, providing critical input to a broad range of tasks while also allowing for a smaller-scale organization. In *Competing in the Age of AI*,[3] Marco Iansiti and Karim Lakhani call on companies to build an "AI factory," which they describe as a "scalable decision engine that powers the digital operating model of the 21st century firm."

Companies must apply AI at scale[4] to unlock the value of data, and they must operate in an agile manner at scale[5] to enable nimble, data-driven teams.

---

3 https://www.amazon.com/Competing-Age-AI-Leadership-Algorithms-ebook/dp/B07MWCTNSD.

4 https://www.bcg.com/publications/2018/big-leap-toward-ai-scale.

5 https://www.bcg.com/publications/2018/big-leap-toward-ai-scale.

Companies also need the right supporting IT infrastructure. They should migrate away from legacy enterprise resource planning (ERP) platforms, with modules that typically are poorly interfaced, toward data management centers of excellence that pool and provide data throughout the organization. Success in this transition will require a strong focus on change management. According to joint BCG and MIT research, a good rule of thumb[6] is to dedicate around 10% of AI investment to algorithms, 20% to technology, and 70% to business process transformation.

Five Principles for Building a Human-Powered AI Company

We believe a successful AI-centered operating model needs to integrate human judgment and experience at its core. Here are five guiding principles to building what we call a "human plus AI" operating model.

1.   **Bring leadership onboard by building the case for change.** Strong leadership commitment is key to successful transformations.[7] One powerful way for the leader of an AI initiative to convince the CEO or board to support bold moves is to demonstrate how little the company is gaining from AI compared with its competitors. A simple acid test: ask the CEO or board members if they can identify at least two critical, strategic processes where the consensus is that AI can make a real difference – an impact of $100 million, say. Then ask if they think the company has made progress on those fronts. Failure to answer yes to both questions means the company isn't doing AI right and dramatic change is needed.

2.   **Reimagine the organization with AI at its core.** Once a company's leadership has come to support bold change, it should consider another disruptive question: How would a new AI-based firm provide the same, or enhanced, value to its customers? Answering that question requires a shift away from the traditional trade-off between scale and marginal costs. Everything should be based on human plus AI – so long as AI adds value. As Alibaba's chief strategy officer, Ming Zeng, has said, "Your firm must enable as many operating decisions as possible to be made by machines fueled by live data."

3.   **Transform into a human-powered AI company.** Even with AI placed at the core, it is crucial to avoid a "zero-human mindset." Indeed, the human role

---

6 https://www.bcg.com/publications/2019/how-to-win-with-artificial-intelligence-ai.
7 https://www.bcg.com/publications/2017/transformations-people-organization-that-work-why.

must be elevated to ensure that there is no area in which AI operates unchecked. Even the most autonomous algorithms and applications need humans to provide the contextual understanding and expertise that AI typically lacks, and to guard against bad judgment or biases. At one point during the COVID-19 crisis, for example, website traffic on a popular British online grocery marketplace soared fourfold. The company's AI-based cybersecurity software interpreted this spike as evidence of a denial-of-service attack and acted to block new transactions. Fortunately, company staff were standing by to correct that mistake.

AI must be augmented by the imagination and interpretation of human beings. Companies should refocus its people on tasks that add the most value, such as designing algorithms, reshaping processes to implement human plus AI integration, strategically monitoring AI inputs and outputs, and engaging in holistic decision making that takes into account second-order implications. A good example of how human plus AI can work together[8] is forecasting in the fashion industry. AI can reduce forecasting errors by 25%, but not all fashion trends can be detected by mining historical data. In our work with one company, we found that combining AI with human expertise could reduce forecasting errors by 50%.

4. **Contain or discard legacy processes.** When reinventing the company for AI, it is important to redesign legacy processes, technology, and organizational structures from the top down. Trying to augment preexisting workflows and legacy ERP platforms by "plugging in" AI is a mistake. Realizing the potential of AI requires consistent, company-wide application. And while the top-down redesign of organizational structures allows for the elimination of unnecessary layers, that doesn't mean everything has to go. Certain applications and infrastructure that have strong interfaces and are able to connect with the central data infrastructure can be retained. But these features should be assessed after the redesign, and the desire to retain them cannot be allowed to influence the transformation.

5. **Prepare people now for the change.** AI systems require a fundamentally different mindset and new capabilities. Preparing employees for change is critical. An absence of leadership and organizational support can cause users to detach, cede responsibility, and avoid risk. Companies must provide employees with on-the-job learning opportunities to master new skills. At a bare minimum,

---

8 https://www.ted.com/talks/sylvain_duranton_how_humans_and_ai_can_work_together_to_create_better_businesses/transcript?language=en.

they must understand what AI can and cannot do so they're able to work with the new technology.

A BCG survey of responses to the COVID-19 crisis found that most companies have focused so far on reactive measures. But now is the perfect time to take bold, transformative action. Companies that have already introduced AI use cases should press ahead immediately in order to achieve maximum impact in the near term. They should not hesitate to scale up, because AI will be a significant lever that can help them manage this crisis. Unless they are digital natives that already have AI at their core, companies should view the current slowdown in day-to-day operations as an opportunity for strategic reflection about how value-creation mechanisms are changing – and how to prepare for the post-crisis world. They should start preparing and reskilling their people and increasing their loyalty, enthusiasm, and long-term value in the coming age of AI.

François Candelon
Chapter 2
How AI-Powered Companies Dodged the Worst Damage from COVID

By the middle of January 2020, AGCO[1] Corp. – the $9 billion American agricultural machinery manufacturer whose brands include Massey Ferguson, Challenger, Fendt, and Valtra – had begun hearing from its suppliers and customers in China about a possible health crisis. That crisis would evolve to become the COVID-19 pandemic.[2] Immediately, AGCO, which has 41 factories, 37 distribution facilities, and thousands of suppliers around the world, turned to an artificial intelligence-based supply chain risk-management system that it had installed in 2015.

The system provides a composite view of AGCO's global supply chain across supplier tiers in real time. By ceaselessly monitoring data on all the risks it has identified, and by continuously analyzing data from hundreds of thousands of online sources and social media, AGCO's AI system is able to flag any vendor that, for any reason, may not be able to deliver components on time.

Using the latest data, the AI-based system predicted – three days before the government announced it – that South Korea would start restricting activity.[3] AGCO was able to accelerate component shipments from that nation before the restrictions took effect. Similarly, the AI system forecast Italy's lockdown[4] seven days before the event, which helped AGCO expedite shipments from its suppliers in northern Italy before they, too, shut down. The AI system's predictions were granular, allowing the company to assign different priorities to suppliers located as close as 50 kilometers from each other. By March 2020, the system's ability to learn and better forecast worsening conditions and rolling lockdowns helped AGCO tackle the crisis in Switzerland, Spain, and Sweden.

As the pandemic begins to ebb across the world, AGCO may be better prepared than its rivals to return to normal because of the AI system. It can help find stockpiles of critical parts, position personal protective equipment (PPE), and identify where the company should focus to expedite the production of critical components. The key issue, though, is whether companies like AGCO will

---

1 https://fortune.com/company/agco/.
2 https://fortune.com/tag/covid-19/.
3 https://fortune.com/2020/05/12/coronavirus-new-cases-china-south-korea/.
4 https://fortune.com/2020/03/08/italy-locks-down-millions-coronavirus/.

https://doi.org/10.1515/9783110775112-002

continue using AI systems to manage the post-pandemic peace as they did during the war on COVID-19 – or whether business will return to viewing the technology as interesting but not essential.

Turning away from AI, which enables machines to solve problems and take actions that only humans once could, would be a grave mistake. The future threatens to be an era of unprecedented uncertainty, with change being the only constant. Political chaos, economic nationalism, trade wars, and extreme weather shifts at the macro level; and changing consumer habits, digitization of products and services, and new ways of working at the micro level were buffeting business even before the pandemic erupted. The COVID-19 crisis only nudged companies – hard – into accepting that the uncertainty tomorrow will be unprecedented, and that the only way to survive is to adopt AI

Using AI in the future will be critical. To manage chronic uncertainty, companies must act on three vectors: They must (1) accurately predict the future to reduce uncertainty; (2) improve their ability to react agilely; and (3) cushion the impact of unforeseen events by being better prepared. AI is an ally for all three. First, AI can develop ultra-granular forecasts that reduce uncertainty. Second, it can analyze the latest data and provide data-driven insights that can optimize decision-making in real time. Third, AI can develop scenarios that will help companies be ready to tackle (almost) anything. Add AI's execution abilities in the form of task automation, and it's easy to see why using AI has become an imperative.

Pioneering AI-savvy companies have already started using the technology to minimize costs and maximize revenues, which is revolutionizing some industries. For example, the $42 billion machinery-maker Caterpillar,[5] is hoping to race ahead of rivals by investing in AI-driven predictive maintenance and autonomous operating technologies. Not only does Caterpillar use AI to reduce its manufacturing and selling costs, but it also markets AI-based services. It installs sensors on customers' earthmoving equipment, even if made by rivals. And, for a fee, customers can license AI-enabled software that will optimize machinery uptime, predict maintenance issues, and operate the equipment 24/7. That's why, in 2019, the Australian mining giant Rio Tinto picked Caterpillar[6] to be the primary provider of hardware and software for its $2.6 billion "intelligent" iron ore mine project in Koodaideri in Western Australia.

It may seem daunting, but CEOs will increasingly have to undertake AI-led digital transformations. Caterpillar, for instance, is reinventing itself as a

---

5 https://fortune.com/company/caterpillar/.
6 https://www.riotinto.com/news/releases/Caterpillar-on-machinery-partnership.

hardware-and-software company instead of remaining a pure hardware manufacturer. Using the Internet of Things, the company plans to collect data in real time from billions of sensors on the 1 million-plus Caterpillar machines that are in operation every day. Cat Digital, its digital technology division, uses AI and digital twins (real-time, virtual representations of physical processes and objects) to learn how customers actually use its products, design better ones, conduct predictive maintenance, and ensure that the equipment works to deliver optimal results. Digital services will be a key driver of the $28 billion in service revenues the company expects in 2026[7] – double the $14 billion it generated in 2016. Caterpillar's digital transformation is reshaping the manner in which the company works with customers and could change the way it creates value tomorrow: From selling hardware and services, Caterpillar may be able to even offer AI-driven customer outcomes such as ultra-granular forecasting of downtimes and highly automated drilling processes.

It's always important to keep in mind that humans will play a key role in AI-driven execution. Their roles will change, and executives will have to learn to work alongside AI, but they will continue to play a major role. From providing input in algorithm design and decision-making rules, to escalating concerns about analyses and applying results across organizations, people will be crucial to capture value from AI During the pandemic, for instance, AGCO Brazil's salespeople used its AI system to figure out how to meet customer orders on time. They modified machine configurations, using locally available components instead of importing them from the US or China. As a result, customers could take delivery of the tractors they needed on time, and AGCO was able to keep its freight costs down – a win-win that was possible only because AI and humans worked together.

History teaches us that global shocks often result in strategic inflection points. They alter the nature of competition, usually in ways that aren't obvious, and the winners are usually companies that act boldly and take risks. The rise of e-commerce giants such as Alibaba and JD.com[8] in China, for instance, was catalyzed by the 2003 SARS outbreak in Asia. In the same way, only companies that reimagine themselves with AI at the core today appear likely to win the post-pandemic future.

---

7 https://www.caterpillar.com/content/caterpillarDotCom/en/news/corporate-press-releases/h/050219_investor_day_announcement.html/.

8 https://fortune.com/company/jd-com/.

François Candelon, Matthieu Gombeaud,
Shervin Khodabandeh

Chapter 3
China's Response to COVID-19 Showed the World How to Make the Most of AI

Soon after Chinese health officials informed the World Health Organization in January 2020 that 41 people in Wuhan had fallen ill with a mysterious pneumonia,[1] China's AI companies started designing or refining their systems and algorithms to fight what would become a global pandemic. In addition to speeding up the deployment of artificial intelligence-based "doctor" chatbots that connect China's rural communities with health care professionals and machine learning algorithms for pharmaceutical research, the AI firms quickly opened four fronts in the then-nascent war on COVID-19[2] – in public health monitoring, medical imaging, robotics, and human-computer interaction.

Several state-owned and private sector AI firms in China – such as 4 Paradigm, Potevio, Airdoc, and Beijing SEEMMO Technology – created AI-based surveillance systems to remotely monitor patients, according to a brief published recently[3] by the Center for Security and Emerging Technology at Georgetown University's Walsh School of Foreign Service. Others – such as Beijing Infervision, Beijing Kunlun Medical, Keya Imaging, United Imaging, and Yitu Technology – incorporated AI into medical imaging technology to detect COVID-19 cases faster.

A third set of firms – including Wuzhu Technology, TMiRob, AUBO Robotics, Keenon Robotics, and Shanghai Mumu Robot – helped minimize exposure to the virus by developing robots that could provide disinfection services, temperature screenings, and contactless meal deliveries in hospitals and medical facilities. And a fourth group – Beijing Unisound, iFlytek, Futong Dongfang, and Yunji Technology, among them – reduced the risk of public transmission by developing voice-based AI systems to ensure less contact with surfaces and humans.

What stands out isn't how China is using AI to tackle the pandemic, but how deep and specialized its health care data, algorithms, and AI research are

---

1 https://fortune.com/2020/02/12/china-coronavirus-experience/.
2 https://fortune.com/tag/covid-19/.
3 https://cset.georgetown.edu/publication/chinas-use-of-ai-in-its-covid-19-response/.

https://doi.org/10.1515/9783110775112-003

becoming in the process. Industry-specific vertical innovation is critical for sustained success with AI, and China's ability to kick-start that cycle in several industries may enable it to take over the leadership of the global AI industry in the not-too-distant future.

To be sure, the US is currently the leader in AI innovation, but China too has combined a treasure trove of data with research, firms, talent, and capital to build a powerful AI ecosystem. The data are revealing: According to Stanford University's *AI Index Report 2021*,[4] China had the largest share of publications in AI journals in 2019, with 18%, followed by the US's 12.3%, and the European Union's 8.6%. In terms of the share of journal citations, China, at 20.7%, overtook the US's 19.8% for the first time in 2019, while the EU lost share at 11%. While China also overtook the US in terms of the number of papers presented at conferences, the US still accounted for 40.1% of conference citations, followed by China at 11.8%, and the EU at 10.9%.

Moreover, China has been pushing AI's use in business as a policy priority that it announced in the *2017 Next Generation Artificial Intelligence Development Plan*. It's rapidly becoming a reality. According to data from the 2020 BCG MIT AI study,[5] Chinese companies may be leading the world in AI adoption. Compared with 45% of companies in non-technology sectors in Europe and 40% in the US, 76% of non-technology companies in China had incorporated AI into processes and offerings by last year. Moreover, 29% reported a transformational impact from using the technology, as compared with 14% in Europe and 13% in the US.

Far-Reaching Economic Consequences

China's growing AI research and its use by business is likely to have two far-reaching consequences.

First, at a micro level, developing myriad AI applications in each industry will lead to continuous AI innovation. That will happen because the AI that solves industry-specific problems requires domain-specific knowledge in order to tackle those problems and to improve over time. The algorithms will gain access to the specialized knowledge they need only if they encounter different problems and are customized to tackle each of them. Thus, AI will generate

---

4 https://aiindex.stanford.edu/report/.
5 https://sloanreview.mit.edu/projects/expanding-ais-impact-with-organizational-learning/?og=Reports+Infinite.

more value as companies learn to use it for different purposes, which will result in segment-specific AI innovations in each industry – as China's health care industry exemplifies. In addition, AI requires constant improvements in the collection of fresh and fine-grained data, so it can learn and perform better over time. As the feedback loops in each segment gather momentum, they will create specialized applications for the industry that will require the development of even more refined AI algorithms.

AI's adoption triggers both innovation and improvement. For instance, AI-based computer vision solutions that were quite generic as recently as few years ago have evolved, among others, into those for autonomous vehicles and those for medical imaging systems. The former focus on distinguishing roads, vehicles, traffic lights, and pedestrians; are sensitive to colors and speeds; and work with lidar systems in real time. The latter control magnetic and radio-frequency pulses; collect and interpret the resulting signals; and transform the data into static MRI images. Both sets of algorithms "see," but do so very differently. Moreover, they must continue to mature in distinctive ways, so they can generate greater benefits in their areas of application.

Second, at the macro level, the widespread adoption of AI will result in companies that are more competitive globally – for several reasons. (1) Corporations will be able to generate more revenues by using AI; the technology can accelerate the pace of innovation and help bring new offerings to market quickly (see, for instance, our earlier *Fortune* column, "At these companies, AI is already driving revenue growth"[6]). (2) AI can create differentiating customer experiences such as personalized pricing and AI-enabled selling. (3) Companies can reduce costs through AI by, for instance, offering predictive maintenance services that reduce machine downtime. Because Chinese companies have been bringing AI products to market quickly and consumers have been willing to adopt them, the country has created an economy that supports AI's evolution.

The implications are clear: Not only should countries and companies drive the adoption of AI in technology-related businesses, but also they must ensure its adoption by non-tech sectors. The latter will make a competitive difference, so governments must focus the development and use of AI in sectors where they enjoy a global advantage. Creating AI ecosystems in key industries by bringing together incumbents, digital giants, startups, venture capital firms, incubators, and academic institutions, and offering support in the form of funding, research institutions, and financial incentives, are logical starting points.

---

6 https://fortune.com/2021/05/07/artificial-intelligence-ai-revenue-growth-netflix-alibaba-spicy-snickers-lancome/.

France, for instance, recently identified four areas of focus for its future AI efforts: Health care, the environment, transportation, and energy. Specifically, the Grenoble region[7] – already a global research and technology center – hopes to become home to AI hubs for both health care and the environment. It has lured 23 corporations, including Atos, Criteo, Google, Huawei, Schneider Electric, and Total; 21 small and medium enterprises; and 11 start-ups to set up AI operations in the region. And the regional government has funded several AI professorships at the University Grenoble Alpes,[8] University Joseph Fourier, and the Grenoble Institute of Technology, laying the foundation for these two promising vertically focused AI ecosystems.

Everyone marvels at China's AI efforts, but the discussion, invariably, turns into a debate about whether the country should be labeled a pioneer or a villain. The real lesson that China's AI experience teaches us is that in the world of artificial intelligence, as in the case of human intellect, it's critical to go a mile wide – and many miles deep.

---

7 https://www.inria.fr/en/centre-inria-grenoble-rhone-alpes.
8 https://miai.univ-grenoble-alpes.fr/en/ai-for-human-beings-environment-799117.kjsp?RH= 6499587984020525.

François Candelon, Georgie Stokol
Chapter 4
At These Companies, AI Is Already Driving Revenue Growth

Four years ago, the $70 billion Alibaba Group, one of the world's biggest artificial intelligence users, teamed up with Mars, the $35 billion global leader in confectioneries, to figure out the types of candy and chocolates that consumers in China prefer. The fresh consumer data that Alibaba continually gathers from the millions of people shopping on its various platforms turned up the counterintuitive finding that many Chinese who buy chocolates also purchase spicy snacks at the same time. Using that data-driven insight, Mars developed a sweet-and-spicy product: a candy bar that contains Szechuan peppercorns, the source of China's spicy "mala" flavor.

Even though Mars didn't conduct any other consumer research to reinforce the AI-driven insight, Spicy Snickers proved to be a winner[1] on the mainland. Depending on AI also saved the company time; instead of the two to three years that it normally takes to launch a product, Mars was able to bring Spicy Snickers to market for the first time in August 2017, less than 12 months after the collaboration with Alibaba started. As a result, Spicy Snickers helped Mars China meet its goal of ensuring that new products should generate 10% of revenues every year.

Using AI to generate revenue – as Mars did in China – still appears to be the exception rather than the rule. It's odd, given that the use of AI applications in everyday life, such as machine translation services, virtual assistants, and automated manufacturing, is proliferating all around us. And the technology's ability to replace human decision-making, which proved to be useful when the COVID-19 crisis[2] engulfed the world last year, has led business to deploy AI to reduce costs and replace employees. But as the post-pandemic recovery takes shape, companies will have to tap into the myriad ways in which AI can boost revenues if they are to get ahead of rivals. Almost 50% of companies have tried, but only 10% are generating significant increases in revenue by using AI, according to the recent 2020 MIT-BCG AI survey[3] of over 2,500 executives.

---

1 https://fortune.com/2018/10/24/alibaba-data-mining-unilever-mars-snickers/.
2 https://fortune.com/tag/covid-19/.
3 https://web-assets.bcg.com/f1/79/cf4f7dce459686cfee20edf3117c/mit-bcg-expanding-ai-impact-with-organizational-learning-oct-2020.pdf.

https://doi.org/10.1515/9783110775112-004

AI can provide companies with the capability to grow revenues in many different ways. Broadly, because AI can improve the accuracy and the granularity of predictions as well as help make real-time decisions, two trajectories become clear: Companies can use AI to generate recommendations that will help executives make better decisions, and/or let AI make decisions and execute them with a minimum of human intervention. The choice will depend on the context; AI is better at analyzing large amounts of data, while humans are more comfortable making decisions in ambiguous contexts.

Where appropriate, it's important to allow AI autonomy while trying to boost revenues, and not deploy it solely to generate insights. Data confirm that: Compared with companies where AI had no, or minimal, impact, those where AI contributed significantly to revenues were 50% more likely to rely on AI-aided human decisions – and 70% more likely to have use cases where AI both made and executed decisions, according to the MIT-BCG survey.

How AI Boosts Revenue

Depending on the extent of autonomy that companies provide AI and the degree of personalization, the technology can help generate revenues in the following ways.

Boosting the Pace of New Product Development

AI helps develop innovative products quickly, as the case of Alibaba-Mars shows. In the same way, Sumitomo[4] Dainippon Pharma teamed up with a British AI-driven firm, Exscientia, two years ago to develop a drug to treat obsessive-compulsive disorder. The startup automated drug discovery[5] by combining data with AI and human expertise all along the development process, from target identification to patient stratification, shortening the preclinical drug discovery stage by 75%. Compared with the industry average of 36 to 48 months, Sumitomo's new drug was ready for clinical trials in just 12 months.

---

4 https://fortune.com/company/sumitomo.
5 https://fortune.com/2018/10/22/artificial-intelligence-ai-healthcare/.

Customizing Recommendations

By using AI, companies can tailor recommendations for all their customers rapidly. Morgan Stanley Wealth Management's[6] advisers, for instance, used to take a minimum of 45 minutes to develop customized investment proposals for clients. By using proprietary AI algorithms, they are able to do so almost instantaneously today. Because of the time savings, each wealth adviser is able to make between five and six additional client calls, on average, every day. The advisers decide if and when to communicate the AI's recommendations, preserving the human touch that clients appreciate.

Taking Personalized Actions

AI can both automate decision-making and take customer-facing actions. For instance, Netflix's algorithms offer each viewer specific recommendations, and they act immediately on the viewer's choice to stream the selected content – there's no human intervention in the process. By offering a range of AI-driven selections, the streaming service tries to win what it calls the Moment of Truth[7] – a two-minute window in which viewers decide whether or not to stay on Netflix. It has found that over 65% of subscribers inevitably choose one of its recommendations.

Personalizing Physical Products

As technologies such as additive manufacturing begin to mature, companies can use AI to create personalized products. Since 2016, the Lancôme division of French personal care products company L'Oréal has been offering Le Teint Particulier, foundation that can be personalized to each user's complexion,[8] which is proving to be a winner. A small AI-enabled machine in a store scans the user's skin, asks for preferences, and then identifies the ideal formulation from 8,000 shades, three coverage levels, and three hydration levels, which combine to make a total of 72,000 possibilities. The machine then mixes the foundation and bottles it for each customer.

---

6 https://www2.deloitte.com/ca/en/pages/financial-services/articles/disrupting-wealth-management-hyper-personalization.html.

7 https://www.lancome-usa.com/le-teint-particulier.html.

8 https://digital.hbs.edu/platform-rctom/submission/netflix-winning-the-moment-of-truth/.

Three Guidelines for Realizing AI's Potential

My experience suggests three guidelines that will help companies augment current revenue streams or search for new ones, thereby realizing AI's full potential:

1. **Keep experimenting to refine your objective function.** Identifying the core algorithm requires iteration. When Netflix launched its recommendations algorithm, for instance, it offered $1 million[9] to anyone who could develop one that would improve its recommendations by 10% or more. The winner turned out to be quite different from the one Netflix had developed, and the company modified its AI accordingly. No wonder Netflix continues to experiment with its algorithm.

2. **Create new revenue streams from your AI capabilities.** Companies can use AI to develop value-added services for existing customers; Rolls-Royce and General Electric[10] have done that by offering predictive maintenance services, which improve the reliability of their aircraft engines. Some, such as insurance giant Ping An, have made money by selling services they initially developed for their own use, such as a fraud detection platform. Still others have used AI to diversify. For instance, Amazon[11] is dipping its toes in the financial services industry,[12] creating new offerings around small- and medium-enterprise payments and loans. It is using its large data sets and AI capabilities to lure consumers away from commercial banks.

3. **Push the boundaries.** Companies must try to develop the most autonomous AI-enabled revenue streams they can if they want to optimize revenues. For example, Rio Tinto[13] is building one of the world's first automated pit-to-port mines in Australia, where it will use AI for scheduling as well as operating decisions. The AI-driven system will boost its revenues by increasing output, speeding up deliveries, and providing better demand forecasts.

Talk about AI, and everyone assumes you're thinking about how to use machines to replace human employees. But that's a stereotypical response; the real power of AI lies in its ability to unleash innovation and accelerate revenue growth. Of course, making that happen will require as much human imagination as it does artificial intelligence.

---

9 https://fortune.com/2009/09/21/box-office-boffo-for-brainiacs-the-netflix-prize/.

10 https://fortune.com/company/general-electric.

11 https://fortune.com/company/amazon-com.

12 https://fortune.com/2018/09/19/amazon-bank-account-prime-bain-survey/.

13 https://www.itnews.com.au/news/rio-tinto-to-build-new-intelligent-mines-494651.

Karen Lellouche Tordjman, François Candelon, Tom Reichert,
Sylvain Duranton, Rodolphe Charme di Carlo, Hind El Bedraoui
Chapter 5
The New Consumer Conversation in an Era
of Uncertainty

Earlier this year, several leading clothing brands saw an unusual spike in sales of tops – but no corresponding increase in sales of skirts or pants. The reason: amid the COVID-19 pandemic, customers were adapting their work wardrobes from office attire to appearances on Zoom and other videoconferencing platforms.

This anecdote is just one illustration of a market-changing trend that has been accelerating for several years, beginning well before the pandemic. Consumer preferences have been evolving rapidly – almost continuously – and have become increasingly volatile, mutable, and uncertain.[1] And they have outpaced companies' traditional abilities to track, anticipate, and respond to trends.

To adapt to what has become "certain uncertainty," companies must find new ways to interact with consumers and gain insight into that uncertainty. It's not as impossible as it might sound. Companies can rely on new "eyes and ears," courtesy of the exploding availability of vast quantities of data from an increasing variety of sources as well as new capabilities afforded by technologies such as artificial intelligence to process, learn, and respond in near real time. These technology advances will enable a new kind of dialogue between companies and consumers that will lead not only to deeper insights into what consumers want but also to a proliferation of offerings from companies seeking to meet consumer needs. We call this emerging model the *new consumer conversation.*

The new consumer conversation will redefine the key success factors for consumer interactions and create substantial competitive advantage. But companies must move fast to be among the first – consumers can't and won't have room for conversations with everyone.

---

1 https://www.itnews.com.au/news/rio-tinto-to-build-new-intelligent-mines-494651.

https://doi.org/10.1515/9783110775112-005

Evolving from Traditional Approaches to Tackle Certain Uncertainty

Traditional interactions between companies and consumers typically rely on a four-step process:

1. **Data Gathering.** First, consumer data (mainly sociodemographic and behavioral data based on past transactions or interactions with the brand, complemented with consumer surveys) is amassed.
2. **Segmentation.** Rules-based techniques such as multivariate regressions are then used to develop differentiated consumer segmentation models. Often, this segmentation remains static for a couple of years, assuming that consumer profiles and preferences conform to a relatively stable structure.
3. **Decision Making.** Based on the segmentation models, marketers and consumer strategy teams make decisions tailored to each segment, from preferred channel choice to product recommendation to message customization.
4. **Implementation.** Finally, the defined decisions are implemented, in the form of an adjusted marketing budget or a new campaign.

This approach is increasingly inadequate because it can't keep pace with the growing volatility of consumer preference and the magnitude of the shifts that result.

A closer look reveals that companies seeking to understand consumer preferences today face challenges from three fronts:

1. The unprecedented rate at which behaviors are shifting is weakening the predictive power of historical data alone. This means predictive models built on historical data must be replaced by near-real-time alternatives, acknowledging shifts and adapting to them as they happen.
2. Uncertain times compound the difficulty of anticipating the pace and magnitude of behavior changes. History provides good examples. The 2008 global financial crisis, for example, led to rapid shifts in consumer buying behaviors, instantly invalidating the traditional equilibrium between price and perceived value.
3. The value of data obtained via consumer surveys has been undermined by the compound effect of long (albeit necessary) time lapses between data gathering and insight generation and by consumers' ever more counterintuitive behaviors in crisis times – behaviors that are often not aligned with their own statements. According to *Jing Daily*, a trade magazine that tracks the Chinese luxury industry, a consumer survey conducted at the peak of the COVID-19 crisis found that 56% of Chinese consumers said they would

spend less on luxury – and yet, one month later, booking volumes for luxury cruises were up 9% among Chinese consumers compared with 2019.

With the emergence of new AI capabilities, companies can circumvent today's growing limitations, opening up new opportunities for consumer interaction. Even just a few years back, companies were forced, for reasons of time and money, to make a trade-off between the size of the audience reached and the variety and depth of the interactions that make up that reach. But AI is a game-changer that is transforming the trade-off into a dynamic feedback loop. With AI at work, intelligent processes happen fast, at scale, and at marginal cost. Lessons learned from a greater volume of interactions enable companies to dynamically update the variety and depth of future interactions. AI is enabling new approaches to consumer interaction that are personalized, self-learning, responsive, and quickly scalable.

Reinventing the Consumer Conversation

The goal for companies now is to engage consumers in the continuously evolving, two-way, and personalized and responsive discussions that constitute the new consumer conversation.

Continuous, Iterative Processes

The new consumer conversation replaces the traditional interactions with iterative and interactive alternatives. The value of treating the interaction as a conversation is that it frames companies' overarching goal – to analyze and respond to shifts in consumer behavior – as a dialogue that allows the company and the consumer to interact on an ongoing basis. This close and continual connection is vital now that consumer behavior has become so mercurial.

These ongoing conversations yield myriad fresh data on consumer behavior. With that insight, and coupled with externally obtained data on macrotrends at work, companies get a more holistic understanding of consumers' preferences and can seek out cues that signal subtle shifts in consumer expectations as they happen. This enables near-real-time self-updating of consumer interactions through continuous learning. Companies are then able to either perfect existing interactions or explore new conversation topics and modes suggested by the cues.

Spotify's new "Shortcuts" feature is an example of how an ongoing consumer conversation can yield fruit. Spotify used vast amounts of data on listening habits, newly released music, and macro musical trends – and leveraged heuristics and machine-learning models – to upgrade the user experience. The result: easier access to an individual's most-used content and a tailored selection of new music to explore. Frequent feedback loops make it possible to constantly improve the experience – recommendations evolve to reflect consumers' listening habits at different times of day, for instance.

Two-Way Connections

Unlike the one-sided approach, the new consumer conversation gives consumers novel ways of interacting that not only allow them to share feedback, content, and opinions but also elevate their contributions by showing them that their input is genuinely in demand and taken into consideration.

Cosmetics brand Glossier has explored such dynamics. The company closely monitors consumers' engagement and commentary on various platforms and constantly iterates with consumers based on these insights. The process unfolds as follows: Looking across platforms at consumer behavior – from purchasing habits to navigation to comments – Glossier identifies interests, whether stated directly or signaled more subtly. Glossier teams build on these insights to produce new content; consumers are encouraged to respond with related, self-created content, such as photos or videos. The Glossier teams then leverage this response from consumers to further refine and personalize content. It's truly a two-sided conversation.

Personalized and Responsive Discussions

Static, pre-established rules once defined companies' interactions with consumers, but the new consumer conversation changes all that through personalization that highlights the individual consumer's wants and needs. This personalization manifests in the tailoring of messages, the choice of conversational tone, the push of services, and the recommendation of particular offerings and promotions.

Consider how a global beverage company is bringing personalization to vending machines. The company is collecting and analyzing massive data sets, including data gleaned from social media, to develop a nuanced understanding of where, when, and how customers consume its products. Then it tailors ads and offerings for individual consumers depending on their current geographic location. The company also links vending machines digitally to the company's smartphone app so that customers can digitally purchase drinks, redeem loyalty program rewards for purchases, and even preorder before arriving at a machine.

Redefining Success Factors

Implementing the new consumer conversation requires a paradigm shift along three fundamental dimensions: new data, new processes, and new decision making (Figure 5.1). Such a shift redefines the key success factors for consumer interactions and emphasizes the urgency of moving from static communication to dynamic conversation.

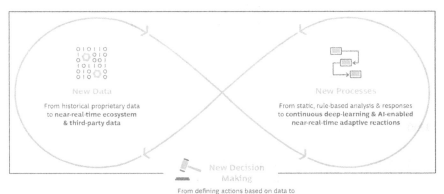

New Data

From historical proprietary data
to near-real-time ecosystem
& third-party data

New Processes

From static, rule-based analysis & responses
to continuous deep-learning & AI-enabled
near-real-time adaptive reactions

New Decision
Making

From defining actions based on data to
defining the rules for AI-based decision making

Source: BCG Henderson Institute.

Figure 5.1: "Certain uncertainty" paves the way for a new consumer conversation.

New Data

The new data that fuels the new consumer conversation is mainly unstructured, coming in large volumes from an ever-broader scope of sources and updated as frequently as possible. As a result, key success factors shift from data quality to data quantity and freshness.

This new data provides companies with the necessary substance to feed the algorithms. They are able to identify even weak signals of consumer behavior shifts and to cope with rapid data obsolescence. For example, a Ben & Jerry's market research initiative leveraged AI and machine-learning capabilities to crunch data from song lyrics and other content. The effort uncovered a new consumer trend: ice cream for breakfast. With this insight, Ben & Jerry's quickly launched breakfast flavors, two years ahead of competitors.

In the course of embracing new data, companies need first to expand their understanding of what qualifies as a relevant data provider and develop a rich ecosystem of new data sources. This means that companies should look beyond digital retailers to access data from broader sources. For example, companies can leverage publicly available data including weather, news, public events, and the evolution of search topics. Aggregating these weak signals can be a valuable asset, helping companies detect strong trends at a fine granularity and then refine a more holistic and comprehensive view of customer habits, preferences, and needs.

Companies also need to ensure data freshness, which has implications for how they access data. That is, companies must build the right data infrastructure for near-real-time sharing with their ecosystem of partners. Finding the right ecosystem of partners is particularly important for industries with low interaction frequency (such as automotive and real estate), because the opportunities for data collection are scarcer.

New Processes

The primary new processes required for the focus on AI-enabled, near-real-time, adaptive reactions, include taking into account the wide set of available data, identifying new patterns, and dynamically personalizing the immediate response to each consumer.

Machine- and deep-learning methods at the core of the new processes create a continuous loop of analysis and action. Each cycle produces new consumer responses and, therefore, new data about consumer behavior. When the system can in turn learn from this outcome data, that new insight fuels the next cycle of action and response. A simple example is Facebook's text-understanding engine, DeepText, which has the functionality to contextually understand not only the content but also the emotional sentiment of thousands of posts to track new hot topics, shifting perspectives on topics, and early signs of discontent. The engine then suggests associated actions, continuously learning from previous interactions.

With these new processes in place, key success factors evolve from the accuracy of analysis to the speed of reaction and learning. With the ever-shorter shelf life of consumer insight, success will be a function of the speed at which companies derive new insights and act on them.

Companies thus need to invest dramatically in AI – from both the technological and the human standpoints. They must remain up to date with fast-moving tech advances. The ability of systems to continuously refine the seamless analysis and action loop is likely to become all the more powerful. Reinforcement learning is a good example: going a step beyond deep learning, it is able not only to draw insights from unstructured data but also to test the effectiveness of its previous insights and autonomously enhance its precision and quality. And from the human standpoint, skilled talent is crucial for companies to master the capabilities and harness the potential of AI.

New Decision Making

In the new consumer conversation, decision making is moving from the last step of the traditional sequential approach toward interaction in order to become an omnipresent and overarching environment within which AI can act in near real time. This new approach to decision making is shifting key success factors from case-by-case decision making to carefully considered and global framing in which AI capabilities and human creative intelligence are synthesized to set the "rules of the game."

As important as AI is to the new consumer conversation, it is also critical to remain mindful of its limits. First, algorithms can introduce bias into consumer behavior analysis by compounding biases already present in input data. Second, AI-based systems can be perceived as off-putting given their power to anticipate needs that consumers themselves may not yet be aware of. Finally, creativity is currently beyond the boundaries of what AI can do. Rather, it relies on the kind of counterfactual thinking – beyond existing data and frameworks – at which humans are best. Thus, AI must be used in conjunction with human input when exploring creativity.

Companies need to carefully track the evolution of the AI systems with human attention and intervention, ensuring the implementation of responsible AI.[2] And companies need to implement the necessary transparency and "tact" – without which consumers might experience personalization as an intrusion or even as a violation of privacy. For example, even if telecoms are able to spot a consumer's interaction with a competing provider, they should refrain from

---

2 https://www.bcg.com/en-us/publications/2020/six-steps-for-socially-responsible-artificial-intelligence.

making contact right away. Instead, they should wait a few days before reaching out subtly with new promotional offers.

Creating New Competitive Advantage

Embracing the new consumer conversation gives companies the opportunity to gain a substantial competitive advantage by breaking the traditional compromise between cost and connection, by fostering hyperresponsiveness and resilience even in uncertain times, and (it almost goes without saying) by creating a greater sense of belonging, affiliation, and engagement among consumers.

Beyond the Cost Versus Connection Compromise

In traditional approaches, and largely because of cost constraints, there was a necessary trade-off between reaching many consumers with a standardized message and reaching few consumers with personalized messages. But with AI at the core of the new consumer conversation, companies can break the traditional trade-off between cost and connection at the interaction level. AI eliminates the requirement to choose between the reach and the richness of interactions by making it possible to, on the one hand, identify new patterns of consumer behavior at unprecedented scale and accuracy and, on the other hand, respond to these patterns in real time. And both come with limited marginal costs.

For example, e-commerce platform eBay partnered with Phrasee, a pioneer of AI-powered copywriting, to generate millions of marketing copies at scale, in just a few clicks. Relying on natural-language generation and deep-learning models, Phrasee's technology is able to generate human-sounding language, customized for eBay's brand voice and adapted to the constantly changing behaviors and preferences of the platform's 100 million email subscribers. Phrasee's technology, operating at scale, also unlocks greater efficiency and lower costs, with each campaign setup requiring only five minutes. In the US alone, the initiative resulted in an uplift of almost 16% in the average open rate and a more than 31% increase in the average click rate, yielding consistent return on investment on all campaigns.

Hyperresponsiveness and Resilience, Even in Uncertain Times

With AI at the core, the new consumer conversation is enabling a hyperresponsive learning loop. It enables companies that embrace it to detect and understand consumer behavior shifts in near real time. It also arms companies to respond not only quickly but adequately to those shifts, pivoting to match new needs and expectations in the most relevant fashion. As a result of this near-real-time responsiveness, companies gain greater relevance and reliability, grounding their resilience in unpredictable times.

With its May 2020 search engine optimization update, Google demonstrated the value of hyperresponsiveness in the context of the high uncertainty surrounding the COVID-19 crisis. Driven by the never-before-seen surge in searches for a single topic over a sustained period, the digital giant updated its search-ranking criteria to reflect users' new definition of relevant content: more-local information, especially on sheltering updates or the latest information on testing, for example.

Greater Consumer Belonging, Affiliation, and Engagement

With their opinions genuinely requested, their needs and preferences thoroughly considered, and conversation topics that extend beyond transaction to match their interests, consumers experience an advantageous "return on relationship investment." They are thus more likely to prefer and proactively interact with brands that, by embracing the new consumer conversation, offer these benefits.

For example, UK-based clothing retailer Asos released an app that allows consumers to upload a photo of a favorite celebrity wearing a coveted outfit. Powered by AI, the app is able to scan the Asos clothing database against the photographed outfit to suggest similar but more affordable products. Such conversation between the consumers and the company resulted in almost 50% more product reviews and increased the likelihood of visitors returning by 75%.

Overall, consumers are more likely to engage when they feel understood, and companies are more likely to succeed when they listen carefully and then respond adequately to consumers' shifting preferences. Such a dynamic creates a new kind of relationship, an evolutionary one in which interactions improve with each interaction. Companies are thus equipped to keep pace with consumer requirements as they shift.

However, consumers cannot and will not invest in too many two-way conversations at the same time. Given that, companies that quickly embrace the new consumer conversation can quickly gain a significant first-mover advantage.

To capture the new competitive advantage, companies must act now along the three dimensions of the necessary paradigm shift in order to successfully implement the new consumer conversation. With this transformation of their consumer interactions, companies will be able to seize a substantial new competitive advantage before others. Importantly, this constitutes an opportunity for incumbent companies to upgrade their consumer interactions to state-of-the-art standards that will no longer be the preserve of digital leaders alone.

François Candelon, Matthieu Gombeaud, Bowen Ding

Chapter 6
Getting the Balance Right: Three Keys to Perfecting the Human-AI Combination for Your Business

After IBM's Watson[1] supercomputer beat the two top-winning *Jeopardy!* champions in 2011, AI seemed ready to take on the world's greatest challenges. Indeed, following Watson's highly publicized quiz show victory, IBM teamed up with some of America's foremost medical institutions to use Watson's algorithms to analyze the vast amounts of cancer data they had amassed, develop data-driven insights, and help health care providers make more effective treatment decisions.

The initiative didn't go as planned. Oncologists turned to AI for answers, but Watson couldn't deliver for various reasons, including gaps and messiness in the data[2] and AI's inability to pick up textual cues in medical documents[3] that were clear to doctors, among others. Several of the cancer initiative's projects eventually shut down.

But the oncologists and engineers in some of the projects took a different tack.[4] Instead of blaming AI for not delivering results, they redesigned the respective roles between human and algorithm. They realized that AI could rapidly cross-reference a patient's genetic profile against the gene mutations mentioned in thousands of digitized academic papers and identify treatments that could have been overlooked. Instead of asking Watson for a solution, they asked it for solution alternatives. In reframing the respective roles of the oncologists and AI, both were able to play to their strengths: the AI reduced the time and effort needed to identify a comprehensive list of potential treatments, while the oncologists used their experience to choose among the treatments and deliver them to patients.

As business increasingly adopts AI, company leaders should keep the lesson of Watson in mind. To generate the optimal results from their investments in AI,

---

1 https://www.ibm.com/ibm/history/ibm100/us/en/icons/watson/.
2 https://www.nytimes.com/2021/07/16/technology/what-happened-ibm-watson.html.
3 https://spectrum.ieee.org/how-ibm-watson-overpromised-and-underdelivered-on-ai-health-care.
4 https://www.nytimes.com/2021/07/16/technology/what-happened-ibm-watson.html.

https://doi.org/10.1515/9783110775112-006

they must understand the different ways in which employees and algorithms can be combined and choose the most effective human-AI combination for the challenge at hand.

Understand the Human-AI Combinations Available to Your Company

Our studies show that there are four templates leaders can follow as they combine employees and AI. These are shown using the Australian mining giant Rio Tinto as an example.

1. *AI as Illuminator:* AI generates data-driven insights to expand the breadth and the depth of employee thinking. Rio Tinto uses algorithms to analyze thousands of drill-core logs and generate 3-D models of ore bodies.[5] This allows exploration teams to better understand the structural configuration of the overall ore deposit and opens new avenues in the search for mineral resources.

2. *AI as Recommender:* AI offers recommendations and employees decide on which ones to act. Rio Tinto uses AI to make predictive maintenance[6] recommendations that its specialists use to create equipment repair schedules.

3. *AI as Decider:* AI makes decisions and employees execute them. Rio Tinto applies machine learning and mathematical programming to make real-time decisions[7] for dispatching the load-haul-dump (LHD) machines at its Argyle Diamond Mine, which are then carried out by human operators.

4. *AI as Automator:* AI makes and executes decisions with employee oversight. Rio Tinto's Pilbara mines in Western Australia have a minimal on-site staff, with most of its engineers remotely overseeing its operations from Perth, 900 miles away. Fully automated, driverless trains[8] carry 28,000 tons of iron ore from the mine to a port 200 miles away.

---

5 https://www.sciencedirect.com/science/article/abs/pii/S0169136815001602.
6 https://www.riotinto.com/about/innovation/artificial-intelligence.
7 https://papers.acg.uwa.edu.au/p/2063_47_Donaldson/.
8 https://www.riotinto.com/en/news/stories/how-did-worlds-biggest-robot.

Use a Decision Tree to Determine the Best Human-AI Combination for Your Application

As Rio Tinto demonstrates, no single combination of employee and AI is inherently superior to another. Instead, executives need to make sound human-AI combination choices by asking themselves questions that clarify the objectives, the context, and the outcomes they expect. Together, these questions, asked in sequence, constitute a decision tree.

- **Objectives:** Do we want to deploy a new business model or improve the efficiency of an existing process? If the former, consider using AI as Illuminator, which will help spur creativity. If it is the latter, the other combinations (Recommender, Decider, or Automator) are better choices.
- **Context:** Do we have data that answers the questions that an employee will ask while solving the problem, and if so, can AI be trained to answer those questions using the data? If the data is available and it can be used to train AI, consider using AI as a Decider or an Automator. If the data is not available or can't be used for training AI, use AI as a Recommender.
- **Outcomes:** Can AI deliver better outcomes than deploying employees? (Typically, this is the case with large-scale, routine processes that require rapid execution.) If the answer to the question is "yes," consider using AI as Automator. If not, use AI only as a Decider.

In addition to these questions, there is an overarching consideration attendant to AI. No matter which human-AI combination companies choose, they must also earn the social license[9] to use AI by designing fair and transparent algorithms, convincing stakeholders that the benefits of AI outweigh costs, and proving it can be trusted with data acquisition and be accountable for AI's decisions. Moreover, as AI evolves and its role shifts from Illuminator to Automator, taking over a greater portion of the decision making and implementation formerly performed by employees, companies will face ever higher hurdles in winning society's approval.

Domino's Pizza offers a good, after-the-fact demonstration of how the decision tree can work. When customers in Australia complained that Domino's products didn't "look good," the company turned to AI. It developed DOM the Pizza Checker,[10] a scanner equipped with computer vision, to compare every pizza that employees make against a database of ideal pizza pictures to ensure

---

9 https://sloanreview.mit.edu/article/ai-at-scale-hinges-on-gaining-a-social-license/.
10 https://dompizzachecker.dominos.com.au/.

that it was visually appealing. Domino's *objective* was to optimize the output of the existing pizza-making process, and a properly trained algorithm was able to do this by checking the appearance of the pizzas (*context*). The pizza-making process is a fast-moving and repetitive process in which product consistency must be ensured at each store, therefore, more time and cost could be saved by using AI-powered robots to execute the entire process (*outcomes*). But it has to be the employees who make (and fix) the product in line with the company's mission of delivering a quality handmade pizza: automating the entire pizza-making process would put Domino's *social license* at risk. This line of reasoning led Domino's Australia to use AI as a Decider.

Regularly Review and Refine Your Human-AI Combinations

The ideal mix of employees and AI evolves along with the technology and company-specific factors, such as objectives, capabilities, and risk tolerances. Thus, executives should periodically revisit the decision tree to ascertain if their human-AI combination is still optimal.

Aircraft engine manufacturer Rolls-Royce uses digital twins and AI to make preventive maintenance recommendations[11] to its customers. Over time its Engine Health Monitoring (EHM) system[12] has become more sophisticated, measuring more performance parameters and feeding richer data streams into its algorithms. As this trend continues, we expect to see the EHM system evolve from a recommendation to decision system, telling airlines when and where to service specific engine parts.

The way in which your company uses AI is no small matter. A recent BCG-MIT study[13] revealed that companies that consider and choose the right human-AI combinations are *six times* more likely to realize significant financial benefits from AI than companies that don't. To unlock the full potential of AI, think about how people and technology will work together.

---

11 https://hub.packtpub.com/how-rolls-royce-is-applying-ai-and-robotics-for-smart-engine-maintenance/.
12 https://www.rolls-royce.com/country-sites/india/discover/2018/data-insight-action-latest.aspx#predictive-maintenance.
13 https://www.bcg.com/publications/2020/is-your-company-embracing-full-potential-of-artificial-intelligence.

Part II: **The Path to Becoming AI-Powered**

Section A: **Data Strategy**

François Candelon, Tom Reichert, Sylvain Duranton,
Rodolphe Charme di Carlo

Chapter 7
Data Alchemy Can Give Decision Making the Golden Touch

The practice of *data alchemy*, which uses continually refreshed, broadly gathered data to find correlations and draw actionable conclusions, has been evolving for several years. But it was only with the pressures of COVID-19, during the "flatten the curve" phase of the pandemic,[1] that this approach became widespread in business. Companies found themselves coping all at once with volatility in workplace dynamics (with the rise of remote working and the cutbacks in budgets and staff), customer engagement, political circumstances, public and private investment, travel and tourism, international supply chains, and health care.

One powerful example of the value of data alchemy is itself related to COVID-19 – and to the Canadian health care risk assessment firm BlueDot, which foresaw the pandemic before just about anyone else. Founded in 2013 to alert governments and businesses to potential infectious-disease outbreaks, BlueDot continually gathered the most recent data from a wide variety of sources: news media in 67 languages, reports on animal and plant diseases, blog entries, airline-ticketing statistics, and social media. It processed all this data through machine-learning algorithms that picked up correlations and patterns that would otherwise be impossible to see.

When BlueDot's algorithms indicated unusual patterns of activity in Wuhan, China, the system automatically brought them to the attention of the company's epidemiologists. On December 31, 2019 – a week before the World Health Organization's first official report – the company published a warning about the COVID-19 virus and its potential impact. Throughout the year, the company continued to correctly predict the spread of the pandemic around the world, projecting its rapid growth in locations like India and Brazil, months before the actual cases and deaths began to climb.

The ability to build a business on this kind of prescience was seen as unusual in the past, attributed to human genius. Now, companies in a wide variety

---

1 https://www.bcg.com/publications/2020/covid-scenario-planning-winning-the-future-series.

https://doi.org/10.1515/9783110775112-007

of industries can deploy a similar ability to see unusual correlations and act on them immediately. The practice of data alchemy is grounded in a new appreciation for what analytics can do, how to use it effectively, and – most importantly – how to embed it in day-to-day decision making.

Introducing Data Alchemy

Although the sweep of change may not yet be evident on a broad scale, it is visible within many companies as they adjust the way they apply analytics. This practice of data alchemy can be summed up in a simple equation with two main components that combine to produce positive decision outcomes (Figure 7.1).

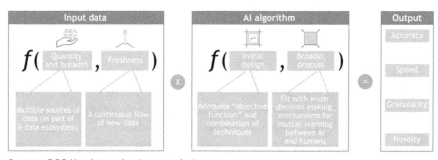

Source: BCG Henderson Institute analysis.

Figure 7.1: The equation for data alchemy.

The first element is the *AI algorithm*, whose logic does not differ from that of traditional use cases. An adequate "objective function" – the formal specification of the problem the algorithm is solving – is identified to optimize decision making. The algorithm may combine different software-engineering techniques, such as natural-language programming, to address the various types of raw data with which it is fed.

The second element is *data*. The enterprise gathers as much data for analysis as possible, regardless of its perceived quality or usefulness. It should not be structured in any particular way; rather, the data should be raw (analyzed without any advance selection or processing), broad (from a wide and ever-increasing variety of sources), and fresh (continually updated and expanded).

This approach to collecting data is critically important because it avoids human bias and preconception. Since no one knows where the weak signals of significant events and insights will come from, there is no such thing as useless data. Returning to a previous example, around 2015, the Ben & Jerry's division of Unilever set its AI-based marketing system to track any references to ice cream in popular culture or on the web. The search seemed dubiously far-ranging and unfocused, until the company found more than 50 popular songs with lyrics referring to "ice cream for breakfast." Suddenly, here was an idea that nobody had recognized, with a built-in market. According to a report on the marketing website Campaign, Stan Sthanunathan, Unilever's head of insights, indicated that Ben & Jerry's used this insight to introduce its own breakfast lineup. He said, "Two years down the road and our competitors are now doing the same."

Anticipating Risk and Opportunity

Already, the full data alchemy approach to decision making is becoming a way of life in many companies. These early adopters of data alchemy are unlikely to go back to their old ways, and others are likely to join them. The power to anticipate upcoming changes amid turbulence, and take advantage of opportunities that would otherwise be unseen, is too great to overlook.

If business leaders expected to keep up their competitiveness, and their cash flow, they would have to make strategic choices more swiftly and with greater granularity and accuracy. Data alchemy provided that means. By comparison, legacy methods of analytics – regardless of whether they use machine learning – are more like conventional gold mining. They simply cannot take place with the same level of granularity, or at any comparable speed, and they lack the predictive capabilities that business leaders are rapidly learning to take for granted.

Other businesses have also found, in the wake of the pandemic, that alchemical capabilities, including those that were begun several years earlier, have given them remarkable levels of resilience. Consider, for example, the predictive analytics system that British Airways built with the Alan Turing Institute (the UK's national data science organization). When COVID-19 struck, the airline was already prepared for one of the most sudden existential crises faced by any industry in history. Not only did airlines lose 75% of their passengers overnight, with no clear idea of when customers would return, but the old methods of scheduling flights rapidly became obsolete.

Travelers now adjust their plans constantly, borders open and close, and the rules for quarantines and social distancing keep shifting without warning. Through "dynamic forecasting," as the Turing Institute calls its form of data alchemy, British Airways can reroute its flights and adjust its ticket prices, according not only to customers' existing travel requests but to the probabilities of newsworthy events, responses to previous price changes, and a wide variety of other proprietary and publicly available data.

Similar forms of data alchemy have helped many other industries as well. Insurance companies have used these methods to assess the coverage risks for small and medium-sized enterprises (SMEs) – after COVID-19 struck, insurers' past performance metrics were no longer accurate indicators. Luxury brands have used scenarios based on data alchemy methods[2] to manage their global inventories, taking into account such seemingly unrelated factors as online searches conducted in East Asia. Logistics firms have used data alchemy to develop higher flexibility in supply chains, an essential quality in a world where threats of tariffs and trade barriers are far more common. In all these cases, and many more, the algorithms routinely recognized and acted upon risks and opportunities that human decision makers would have missed.

Beyond AI-Enabled Gold Mining

In fairly stable and predictable business environments, gold mining was adequate even with its inherent limitations. Company decision makers knew what information they were looking for and could plan for the time needed to find and refine the data. Because the range of potential strategic paths forward was constrained, business leaders didn't worry about what they *weren't* looking for with data gold mining. Rather, they chose to analyze the nuggets of information that seemed most relevant to the critical problems at hand.

But now, in this more turbulent era, many companies have begun to use AI and big data in order to optimize their gold-mining processes. When introducing a new product, for example, they might conduct market research and customer sentiment analyses to build forecasts, with machine learning in place to refine the forecasts.

Because it takes time to select sources, data gold mining produces results more slowly than data alchemy (Figure 7.2). Moreover, gold mining processes a limited selection of data that is inherently prone to bias, owing to the way it is selected. This gives gold mining a relatively low predictive capability.

Combining AI and the gold-mining approach addresses these concerns to some extent. Using a now familiar example, when the Mars global confectionary

---

2 https://www.bcg.com/publications/2020/win-covid-19-battle-with-scenarios.

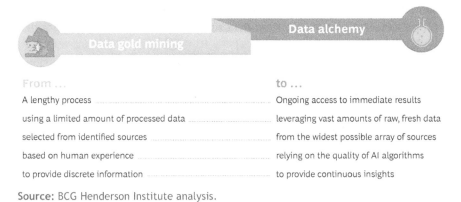

From ...	to ...
A lengthy process	Ongoing access to immediate results
using a limited amount of processed data	leveraging vast amounts of raw, fresh data
selected from identified sources	from the widest possible array of sources
based on human experience	relying on the quality of AI algorithms
to provide discrete information	to provide continuous insights

Source: BCG Henderson Institute analysis.

Figure 7.2: Comparing data gold mining with data alchemy.

business partnered with the Tmall Innovation Center (the market research division of the Chinese e-tailer Tmall), Mars used an AI-enabled approach to analyze purchased data from Tmall's 500 million users in China, intending to reduce the risk of product development failures. An analysis of historical snack purchase information alerted Mars to trends in local consumer preferences, so the company brought the Spicy Snickers candy bar to market. It was an immediate hit. But even this success represented a somewhat limited improvement compared with the greater opportunities that the company might have found with a broader sweep of data – if it had gone beyond gold mining to a full implementation of data alchemy.

Even in their use of AI, most business decision makers have relied on the gold-mining approach. But in the COVID-19 era of increased volatility, gold mining is less and less viable. Simply put, decision making based on experience – relying on past data (such as human-led promotional campaigns or machine learning trained on a well-defined earlier data set) – is now obsolete. Companies are better off practicing data alchemy and, considering the level of uncertainty and unpredictability in today's world, alchemy is likely to be a perennial practice in many companies.

In China, for example, Ant Financial (a subsidiary of Alibaba) opted for an alchemy approach in granting loans to Chinese SMEs. The company developed an algorithm that provides a decision for each routine loan application, including the interest rate to offer. The algorithm continually refines itself, relying on a steady stream of fresh data, with billions of activity inputs replenished from more than 3,000 sources of activity throughout the Alibaba system, including popular e-commerce platforms like Taobao. The percentage of defaults is less than 1% – lower than a firm would obtain with a gold-mining paradigm – and will presumably drop even further over time as the accuracy of the algorithm continues to improve.

Ant Financial has also adopted data alchemy as the core logic of its business model and the source of its competitive advantage. By promoting its 3-1-0 model directly to customers (3 minutes to fill in the application, 1 second to get an answer, and no time after that to receive funds, with zero human intervention), the company has reached the point where it holds loans for more than 50% of all Chinese SMEs.

Had Ant gone with a traditional gold-mining approach, it would have based its loan-granting decisions on analysis (by humans, software, or machine learning) of the past credentials and forecasted business outlooks for each applicant. This analysis would not be reliable, because of the rate and magnitude of change in business operations today, particularly in relation to COVID-19. Past performance is not a predictor of future financial situations.

The practice of data alchemy, though it may seem unfamiliar at first, is accessible and scalable. It is not just the province of digital natives. On the contrary, a growing number of traditional companies are making the shift and updating their decision-making processes accordingly. For example, traditional insurance companies increasingly rely on data alchemy when underwriting policies. Why? Because – as highlighted by the pandemic – the traditional analyses of potential business losses, using selected data such as past years' financial results, are inadequate. Alchemy has enabled insurers to make extensive changes in their internal decision-making processes; for instance, they can streamline multiple decision layers into a more rapid, seamless process. It also changes their externally facing procedures, such as the handling of customer interactions.

A Stronger Role for People

When AI is introduced, concerns often arise regarding the implications for people. Figure 7.3 depicts the function of human decision makers in the data alchemy equation. People play four critical roles: building the data ecosystem, designing the algorithm and the process around it, selectively monitoring the output for bias and other anomalies, and managing exceptions flagged by the system.

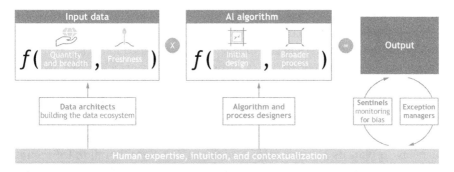

Source: BCG Henderson Institute analysis.

Figure 7.3: A new role for humans in data alchemy.

Data Architects

People play a fundamental role in building the digital ecosystem to gather as much data as possible. They set up an architecture that ensures a constant flow of fresh data from the widest possible array of sources. These include a variety of external wellsprings: publicly accessible data from internet searches, purchased-access databases and information marketplaces, and proprietary records shared by other companies within a data-sharing ecosystem. Some companies also have internal sources, resident within a firm's own data lake and analyzed together with external data.

Algorithm and Process Designers

The skills of AI specialists, already highly sought-after in the labor market, are particularly relevant to data alchemy. The design of the algorithm is key to success. And this is only one part of a broader decision-making process that must be entirely reinvented with AI at its core. Only skilled human experts, with technical and business capabilities at their disposal, have the knowledge and creativity to design and implement an alchemical system.

Sentinels

The companies benefiting the most from AI are those where humans and machines learn from one another. That was the primary conclusion of *Expanding*

AI's Impact with Organizational Learning,[3] the 2020 annual study by the BCG-MIT Artificial Intelligence Global Executive Study and Research Project. Hence the need for sentinels: data scientists who continually pay attention to algorithms in order to investigate suspected biases and make adjustments when required. For example, sentinels may detect cases where the algorithm consistently produces outputs that have a low level of accuracy or where it lacks insight about the appropriate context.

One such situation occurred when a European apparel company used data alchemy to plan its January sales campaign. The algorithm didn't discount Christmas-themed sweaters because they had been very popular during the previous month. People on the marketing team understood the context that the algorithm did not: the holiday market is only temporary. Once humans noticed this problem, they rapidly adjusted the algorithm to account for this context in all future holiday sales.

Exception Managers

Some executives are concerned that data alchemy will force them to relinquish control over their decisions. In fact, the opposite is true. Data alchemy frees up their attention for the decisions that require in-depth consideration. The algorithm makes all routine choices, but whenever it flags something (such as a low level of confidence in an outcome or a decision with major strategic implications), human managers step in and set the course, using their expertise and intuition. For example, in underwriting policies, an insurance company's algorithm worked mostly autonomously. It would flag cases for escalation only when the margin of error rose above a preset threshold or the amount of money at stake exceeded an agreed-upon financial value. For the human underwriter, the benefits are clear: less time on routine but necessary busywork for simple claims and more time to investigate the complex, challenging cases and consider their strategic implications.

Becoming an Alchemist

In the years to come, the level of uncertainty and unpredictability in the business environment is unlikely to decrease; however, data alchemy will not be a

---

3 https://sloanreview.mit.edu/projects/expanding-ais-impact-with-organizational-learning/.

short-lived trend. Because it enables faster, more granular, and more accurate decisions, it is bound to lead to permanent changes in decision-making mechanisms – both for incumbent companies and for digital natives.

So where should you start? Across your organization, identify important decisions where the level of accuracy has recently dropped, owing to the unprecedented speed and magnitude of the change you have been facing. This is a key indicator that a shift to data alchemy would be valuable. If you also sense that you no longer have all the elements in hand to make a sound decision, this is an additional red flag. Bear in mind: if you identify this need, your competitors will likely do so as well. And because data alchemy can become a source of competitive advantage, it's urgent that you act before others do.

Massimo Russo, Tian Feng
Chapter 8
How Far Can Your Data Go?

A few years ago, the idea that data was the new oil caught on. As consumers revealed more of their behaviors, preferences, and attitudes via their electronic devices, companies realized that data, too, is a plentiful, tradeable, and highly valuable commodity.

But data has distinct characteristics that make it very different from oil – or any other commodity. For one thing, the array of sources and amount of supply are virtually infinite. For another, data can be used (or consumed) more than once, and it can be used in multiple places by multiple parties at the same time. Moreover, while it's hard to hide a tanker full of oil, it's easy to mask a few billion bytes of data – and then put them to uses (beneficial or nefarious) without the awareness of the original data generators. Data is also unlike most commodities in that different types can have different value, and sometimes that value is not immediately clear. Finally, data can be used for lots of different purposes, many of which were neither contemplated nor intended when the data was first generated. We call these "alternative data uses."

The myriad alternative uses of data, the ease with which it can be replicated and shared indefinitely at no cost, and the trillions of bytes of data coming on-stream from the Internet of Things (IoT) pose big and far-reaching questions with respect to ownership, privacy, and value.[1] B2B enterprise data sharing, in particular, is just starting to take these issues into account. As companies prospect for new sources of value, the rules, standards, and conventions governing data ownership rights and the regulatory frameworks for privacy and data sharing have yet to take shape.

In this chapter, we take a tour of the alternative data use landscape and offer some thoughts for business executives who want to realize value from what will be the dominant resource of the 21st century. How should companies think about use cases that are unknown or do not yet exist? How can they balance the abstract value of future use cases with the actual risk of data misuse?

---

1 https://www.bcg.com/publications/2020/imperative-of-data-privacy-plans-for-b2b-compa nies-part-4.

https://doi.org/10.1515/9783110775112-008

Collective Value/Private Risk

It's impossible to overestimate the number of potential sources of IoT data and the endless possible combinations of data from those sources. (By 2025, the volume of data from IoT devices will reach almost 80 billion terabytes, according to International Data Corporation (IDC) estimates.) On a typical city block, sensors on numerous data entities generate data that can be recombined for use in countless areas, such as mobility, public safety, economic development, and health care. This data travels through complex webs of intermediaries leading from the source to the ultimate users and applications.

But the use cases that companies have pursued so far are mostly limited to a fruitful but restricted set of opportunities, typically involving players within a single industry. Increasingly, however, companies are starting to move from using their own data to improve internal processes or products to developing applications that require participation in an ecosystem or some form of cross-entity or multi-industry data sharing. Shared data can lead to deeper insights into customers or operations, and data provided to an ecosystem that combines data from multiple sources[2] can enable entirely new applications. One benefit of ecosystems is that the collective contributions of the participants can accomplish more than any individual company could do on its own. They drive innovation and collective value.

The common tools employed by today's data-sharing ecosystems – such as application programming interfaces and data licenses – control, monitor, and limit data use; and a big part of their job is to mitigate risk. The deeper a company ventures into data sharing and the further afield it ventures from the business it understands best, the more control it must cede to others and the more uncertainty it must endure. While companies can often easily capture the value from data applications linked to their core businesses, it is more difficult to identify and capture the value of distant and novel applications. Risks related to both losing control of data and realizing value from data[3] rise in significance. Collective value and private risk can come into conflict (Figure 8.1).

---

2 https://www.bcg.com/publications/2020/value-in-iot-platform-based-business-models.
3 https://www.bcg.com/publications/2020/innovation-data-1.

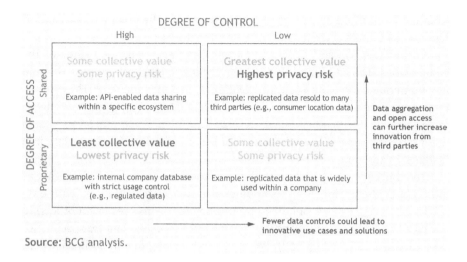

Source: BCG analysis.

Figure 8.1: Collective value and private risk in data sharing.

Three Features of Alternative Data Uses

Many alternative data uses share three features that distinguish them from more predictable use cases.

First, alternative uses are often developed after the data has been collected or combined and are therefore difficult to predict. For example, the Automatic Identification System, originally intended to track the location and identity of ships in order to reduce collisions, is now the source of data used in applications from economic analysis and insurance to oceanic research. Similarly, the strategic logic of IBM's acquisition of the Weather Company may not have been obvious on the surface, but weather data can be used in a wide range of applications in such industries as agriculture, aviation, construction, and logistics; as well as in more distant applications in health care, finance, insurance, retail, and utilities. The Weather Company's copious data generation capability augmented IBM's ability to better serve its customers with cloud applications in those and other industries.

The second distinguishing feature of alternative data uses is that they often occur in applications far from the original source of the data, which may pass through a series of intermediaries before it is put to work. Scrubbed, restructured, aggregated, analyzed, and distributed (to potential additional aggregators), the data comes into contact with a complicated web of players. This enables it to get from the point of origin to distant applications, but the process also makes it hard for the owners of the data to track its ultimate uses.

Copenhagen's experience setting up its City Data Exchange highlights the complexities. The city found that not only will a single data set pass through many intermediaries, but each intermediary transforms the data. These transformations take place for several reasons. Some data is fragmented and needs to be aggregated with other data to develop a solution. Some generators of data don't have the capabilities and analytical skills needed to transform data into insights. In addition, different use cases require different forms of processing.

The third feature of alternative data use cases is that they are increasing as more applications shift from technology-driven "push" solutions (with data producers or aggregators building applications for themselves or for others) to use case-driven "pull" solutions (with companies sourcing data for specific use cases that they have identified). We are already seeing this trend in smart cities,[4] where governments are blending data to fashion more citizen-centric services. One example is the variety of new IoT solutions that are helping people stay independent and connected as they get older. Wearables and room sensors can alert emergency services if an accident occurs in an elderly person's home, which makes living alone safer and alleviates the worry of friends and family. Exercise equipment combined with mapping data can help prevent memory loss. Electricity- and water-metering data, originally designed to monitor utility use, can be used to assess activity in a residence and alert social workers in the event of a sudden drop-off.

Monetizing Alternative Data Uses

Alternative data uses are still relatively uncommon, in part because the path to monetization for the data owners often isn't clear. Our experience and research have identified seven reasons why companies can be reluctant to monetize data:

1. **Lack of Imagination.** The companies that generate and own the data simply cannot imagine its value generation potential, especially when it lies far from their core business or industry.

---

4 https://www.bcg.com/publications/2020/smart-cities-need-to-understand-the-risks-and-rewards-of-data-sharing-part-3.

2. **Unknown or Unidentifiable Value.** The data's value may depend on awareness of its alternative uses or on access to data from other alternative sources, making it difficult for companies to price their own data.
3. **Fear of Losing Value.** Companies recognize the potential for future valuable use cases but worry that sharing data with partners may undermine their ability to capture its value themselves.
4. **Fear of Losing Control.** Given data's complicated journey from origin to application, companies fear that sharing their data may cost them control of its ultimate uses – and bring attendant financial, brand, or regulatory risks.
5. **Data Platform Limitations.** Companies' technological ability to stream, track, control, and ultimately charge and get paid for their data is limited.
6. **Contractual Limitations.** Companies are constrained by contractual terms from monetizing data originally generated by their customers.
7. **Limited Data Inventory and Quality.** Companies do not know what data they own or whether it is of sufficient quality to be useful.

Times are changing quickly, however, and corporate and other data users are overcoming these constraints. For example, BCG has been advising three very different organizations – an automotive OEM, a large commercial trucking company, and a municipal government – on how they can extract value from alterative data uses. All three are following a similar roadmap and process.

They catalogue their data internally to get the best sense of what is available. Like other leading explorers of alternative data uses that emulate digital natives such as Airbnb, Uber, and LinkedIn, these organizations maintain data catalogs that make their data readily available to internal and potentially external users. New data management platforms, such as Talend and Collibra, help sort data to make it more accessible.

They establish processes to think creatively about the value of their data. Conceiving of use cases in adjacent industries is easier, but these organizations pushed themselves to consider the needs of other sectors and the broader economy. They revisit this thinking as use cases enabled by new technologies emerge.

They seek partners that can augment their own capabilities and overcome limitations. Sharing data to find new use cases doesn't just divide the pie, it can enlarge the pie. And while a company may hold a very valuable data set, it may not have the capabilities or market position to make the most valuable use of it. It's important to find the right partners and to understand the different ecosystems that could benefit from the data and the potential solutions that other companies could contribute.

They keep an eye out for changing data uses. IoT and artificial intelligence are continually evolving, so identifying opportunities to monetize data is not a one-time exercise. Companies can establish a formal process, with external advisors and partners, to stay current on how data can be used across a broad range of industries.

They carefully balance opening their data to discovery against exposing it to excessive risk. Holding data too tightly may deprive a company of a revenue stream and society of valuable use cases. But sharing it too broadly may have unintended consequences. A number of methods exist to balance this trade-off, including data directories, sample data sets, synthetic data, and distributed data models that allow access but prevent the data from being replicated.

Albert Einstein used thought experiments to visualize his theories and understand an untested theory's implications in the physical world. Business leaders may want to use a similar technique to visualize how their data can be used. Like alternative data uses themselves, such experiments may fall outside of normal management practices, but the companies that are first to understand the value of alternative data – and how to realize it – can build new revenue streams and new sources of competitive advantage.

François Candelon, Massimo Russo, Rodolphe Charme di
Carlo, Hind El Bedraoui, Tian Feng

Chapter 9
Simple Governance for Data Ecosystems

As big companies explore new revenue streams and business models based on data, they quickly run into a quandary. On the one hand, combining the data they control with data from other sources significantly increases the number and value of potential available use cases. On the other, that same act of data sharing opens up issues of trust and misuse, lost value, and unrealized opportunity. In many cases, the potential risks (which tend to be more readily identifiable) appear to outweigh the prospective rewards (which are often more distant and uncertain), and the companies proceed no further. This is unfortunate, understandable, and unnecessary.

Data sharing –particularly the exchange of the exploding quantities of data generated by the Internet of Things –has emerged as an important and high-value commercial activity. It can help advance new business models, drive innovation, and tackle some of society's most pressing challenges, such as making cities more efficient and livable. Data sharing is facilitated by data ecosystems comprising multiple parties within and outside of an individual company's industry. These ecosystems can overcome some major barriers to data sharing, including the unclear value of data at the point of generation and the need for collective intelligence to identify and match participants with opportunities for value creation. Broadly, data ecosystems are important vehicles for aligning companies around common goals while giving them the agility needed to innovate.

For the orchestrators of data ecosystems –which can be tech companies, large industrial incumbents, or innovative startups –the stakes are high: if other companies are not willing to share their data, the ecosystem dies on the vine. Still, many companies continue to hoard their data –to their own detriment and that of the ecosystem as a whole.

Simple and effective rules of governance can help break the data gridlock. But in the face of many possible design choices, companies don't always know where to start. A good first step is to understand that data sharing in an ecosystem is fundamentally an issue of cooperation, with rules guiding good behavior and setting the terms of engagement. BCG's Smart Simplicity framework,[1] which

---

1 https://www.bcg.com/en-us/capabilities/organization/smart-simplicity.

https://doi.org/10.1515/9783110775112-009

is designed to help companies make sense of organizational complexity and encourage cooperation, can help.

The Sources of Data Gridlock

Our research and client experience show that problems with data sharing generally revolve around four issues: trust and privacy, transaction costs, competitive concerns, and worries over missed or lost financial opportunity (Figure 9.1).

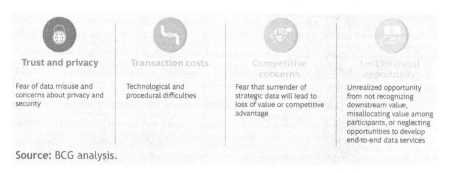

Trust and privacy	Transaction costs	Competitive concerns	Lost financial opportunity
Fear of data misuse and concerns about privacy and security	Technological and procedural difficulties	Fear that surrender of strategic data will lead to loss of value or competitive advantage	Unrealized opportunity from not recognizing downstream value, misallocating value among participants, or neglecting opportunities to develop end-to-end data services

Source: BCG analysis.

Figure 9.1: Four barriers impede data sharing.

1. **Trust and Privacy.** This barrier is rooted in the fear that data will be mishandled, misused, or mis-shared. Poor technology, weak governance, and actual data breaches can all lead to data being used for purposes that were not agreed upon by the originator of the data and others in the ecosystem.
2. **Transaction Costs.** These costs underlie every data exchange, and problems can be both technological and procedural in nature. Technological impediments include poor connectivity, mismatched standards, and constraints on interoperability. Procedural barriers can involve mismatched skills, organizational complexity, or ambiguous rules. Technological advances such as 5G mobile connectivity, better industry standards, broker platforms, and data fusion tools are emerging to tackle the former. Sharing governance can tackle the latter. But as more heterogeneous IoT data comes online, new challenges are likely.
3. **Competitive Concerns.** The data landscape is still mostly unmapped, and new, unforeseen use cases appear every day. Companies rightly fear surrendering competitive advantage along with strategic data. Incumbent contributors to an ecosystem may worry that competitively sensitive information will

be released to rivals. New digital entrants may worry about digital giants copying their tools or poaching their talent. All participants may worry about ecosystem orchestrators capturing a disproportionate portion of the value.

4. **Lost Financial Opportunity.** Another ramification of the unmapped landscape is the possibility that sharing data may cause financial opportunities to be overlooked. This could result from a failure to recognize data's downstream value, from misallocation of value among an ecosystem's participants, or from neglected opportunities to develop end-to-end data services internally. For example, vendors and customers can work together to coordinate logistics, rationalize inventory, and even codesign products, but the benefits and investments may not accrue evenly across the supply chain.

If the barriers to sharing are sufficiently high, they will cause *data gridlock*. A 2018 European Commission study found that of 129 companies surveyed, 60% did not share data with other companies and 58% did not reuse data obtained from other companies. When gridlock occurs, data ecosystems fail to thrive and value creation is limited.

Overcoming Gridlock

Two successful European ventures demonstrate how to overcome the barriers to data sharing and break out of gridlock. Their operations and data are now global in scale.

HERE Technologies

Owned by a consortium of German auto OEMs (original equipment manufacturers) and Tier 1 suppliers (including Intel, Mitsubishi, and NTT, among others), HERE is the world's leading location data and technology platform provider, supporting data sharing at scale through both its core data offering and its marketplace platform. The company sources data from thousands of independent contributors and partners, including the OEMs themselves –which, as owners, are able to capture the residual value of HERE's operations. The company provides recommended standards, pools data, and provides scale and reach via aggregated data services, thus facilitating coordination and reducing the fear among the consortium's participants of any competitive disadvantage that might exist if a single company led the venture. HERE Marketplace connects data sources (providers) with data consumers (buyers) and supports the former in assessing the value of their data and capturing it through potential use cases. The private marketplace's features reassure data providers that they control access to and use of their data.

To facilitate data sharing, HERE provides an intuitive user experience and a suite of APIs (application programming interfaces) and software development kits, as well as a set of data monetization services. Compliance with the EU's General Data Protection Regulation (GDPR) and a comprehensive privacy charter ensure approved and acceptable data use. The partner-vetting process and blockchain-based consent management system give data users and data contributors confidence that their personally identifiable information will be shared only with service providers they approve of and only once that approval is in place.

In addition to highlighting commercial use cases for data, HERE emphasizes the value of data sharing through public-service projects such as the EU Data Task Force, no-fee exchange of data shared under Creative Commons licensing, and its multiple customer- and partner-led COVID-19 response efforts.

Airbus Skywise

Launched in 2017, Airbus's Skywise open platform is an integrated service and data solution leveraging a data analytics software suite that helps airlines analyze aircraft data collected by sensors while planes are in flight and on the ground. Skywise now includes more than 100 airline partners –regional airlines, global giants, and industry rivals (Delta and United are both members) – that share data with the goal of improving operations.

Airbus maintains that each airline owns its data. In exchange for sharing, participants gain access to Skywise analytics insights and benchmarking data. The company also publishes success stories that illustrate the value of participation. To manage competitive concerns, Airbus ensures that only aggregated benchmarks are shared among contributors.

Because most of the sensor data is generated by Airbus planes and their flight data is similar, Airbus is able to transform data from different airlines into a standard format. GDPR compliance sets a baseline level of acceptable data use, and a publicized partner-vetting process provides transparency around data access.

Data Ecosystem Participants

In both of these examples, the companies involved overcame barriers to data sharing by setting up built-for-purpose ecosystems with clear rules of governance. Such ecosystems organize the data assets and customer connections of a group of business partners in order to deliver new products and services – both within and across traditional industry verticals.

Data ecosystems have three types of participant. *Orchestrators* (such as HERE and Airbus) set the rules, coordinate the activities of the other participants, aggregate their data and expertise, and deliver a range of products or services to the end customer. *Contributors*, which may be participants in multiple ecosystems, provide their data and services or build and sell applications with the help of the ecosystem's data. *Enablers* provide infrastructure for the ecosystem, including connectivity, security, and computing power.

Orchestrators cannot orchestrate unless they create the right context for breaking through the data-sharing gridlock and encouraging cooperation. Like employees who must decide whether it's worth their while to work together on a risky project, companies embarking on data sharing must assess the value, risk, and potential conflicts involved. This is where good governance can help.

Smart Simplicity Rules of Governance

BCG's Smart Simplicity approach promotes such cooperation within complex organizations. Instead of crafting rules one by one to target specific behaviors, Smart Simplicity explores the context underlying a system of behaviors by analyzing the motivations of individuals. It then uses six simple rules to change the context (Figure 9.2).

The first three rules help organizations create the conditions for individual autonomy and empowerment. The other three compel people to confront complexity and cooperate with others so that the overall performance of the organization –in this case, the data ecosystem –becomes as important to them as their own individual performance. Of course, there are additional rules[2] that ecosystem orchestrators will need to consider regarding data ownership, access, and use, but those will vary by ecosystem.

Rule 1. Understand what people really do. To untangle the competitive and trust barriers within an ecosystem, orchestrators need to understand the goals,

---

2 https://www.bcg.com/en-us/publications/2020/how-do-you-design-a-business-ecosystem.

		Barriers addressed			
		Trust and privacy	Transaction costs	Competitive concerns	Lost financial opportunity
1 Understand what people really do	Map agents, goals, resources, and barriers	●	●	●	●
2 Reinforce the integrators	Define standards		●		
	Create sharing pipeline and infrastructure		●		
3 Increase the total quantity of power	Create 360 data use and sharing rules	●		●	
	Signal noncompetition			●	
	Define clear default rules	●	●	●	
	Define standards of good behavior	●		●	
4 Increase reciprocity	Define the mutual interest in sharing data	●		●	●
	Publicize valuable use cases				●
5 Expand the shadow of the future	Design value creation and sharing model			●	●
6 Reward those who cooperate	Assign financial value to data shared				●
	Create recognition system for data contributors				●

Source: BCG analysis.

Figure 9.2: Six rules of the smart simplicity data sharing approach.

resources, and constraints of its participants. Such an understanding helps orchestrators design governance measures that address the underlying motivations of ecosystem participants, not just their behaviors.

Rule 2. Reinforce the integrators. In data ecosystems, the orchestrators and enablers often play the role of integrators –participants whose influence makes a difference in the work of others. Integrators bring others together and drive processes. They work at the nexus where constraints and requirements often meet. Defining standards by generating and sharing the same data formats, using the same protocols, and following the same reference architecture can lower barriers to data sharing. Organizations such as the International Data Spaces Association are exploring standards to make data sharing seamless. Creating pipelines and infrastructure (APIs, for example) that facilitate sharing can also reduce friction.

Rule 3. Increase the total quantity of power. Empowering people to make decisions without taking power away from others is a great way to make sure all participants feel they have a stake in the ecosystem's success. Orchestrators have several ways to do this. Access controls, 360-degree sharing rules, and rights management can build confidence that contributors' data will be used in the right ways, even as it moves out of the hands of the orchestrator. Providing transparency into the sources and uses of data, and giving contributors a role in deciding how their data will be used, can also help. A good example is the privacy settings on Apple's iPhone, which give users the ability to determine which applications can access which data streams.

Being explicit about the ecosystem's strategic positioning in the market and implementing noncompete agreements among participants can reduce competitive barriers and give contributors peace of mind about sharing sensitive data. Privacy-preserving analytical tools that protect the underlying data while others analyze it give participants further confidence that their data is secure.

Making clear the ecosystem's default position on such issues as data ownership and usage control also promotes sharing and reduces concerns arising from ambiguity. Data ecosystems need clear standards of acceptable and unacceptable behavior. Data capture without consent, data sharing with competitors, and unauthorized resale to third parties should be clearly off-limits. Orchestrators can support monitoring and enforcement of these norms.

Rule 4. Increase reciprocity. The success of each participant in the ecosystem depends on the success of others. To drive this home, orchestrators should clearly define participants' common purpose and their mutual interest in sharing data. The clearer the purpose, especially in the absence of defined contractual terms, the more readily will the ecosystem's individual contributors move in the desired direction and avoid improper behavior. Orchestrators can also publicize successful use cases. At its annual LiveWorx conference, for example, IoT tech enabler PTC runs demonstrations of collaboration unlocked by its SaaS (software as a service) data-sharing tools.

Rule 5. Expand the shadow of the future. A good value creation and sharing model shows people how their success is furthered by contributing to the success of others. And the same goes for fairly sharing the value that results, whether financial or some other benefit. For example, precision agriculture ecosystems often have a clear value proposition: share machinery data and we will give you the resources needed to improve your yields. Ecosystems that do not share value fairly soon find that they must rethink their model or fall apart.

Rule 6. Reward those who cooperate. There are at least two ways that orchestrators can create a recognition system for data contributors. One is to assign a financial value to the data shared; the other is to link some form of nonfinancial remuneration to data sharing. In some successful data ecosystems, sharing data is regarded as a good in and of itself, with the value created often linked to social as well as economic goals. New York University's GovLab has created a list of more than 200 data collaboratives that share data for public value. Similarly, companies such as Microsoft are promoting the idea of open data sharing. Orchestrators and contributors may be able to use their participation in data-sharing ecosystems to support their social-impact goals and reporting.

Ecosystems are emerging as promising vehicles for data sharing. Yet the cooperation necessary for their adoption at scale is still limited, hampered by issues of trust and privacy, transaction costs, competitive concerns, and worries over missed or lost financial opportunity. For data ecosystems to break out of data-sharing gridlock, they need to maximize value creation for all stakeholders while mitigating the risks and ensuring a safe space for exploration and learning. Smart, simple data governance measures, in partnership with technology, are key tools for enriching the data economy.

Massimo Russo, Tian Feng
Chapter 10
What B2B Can Learn from B2C About Data Privacy and Sharing

Concerns about the sharing of data from digital activities and devices typically focus on consumer privacy. COVID-19 and the much discussed need for a public-health response that includes widespread, automated contact tracing has brought these issues into sharp relief.

The benefits of the ability to track those who have been exposed to the novel coronavirus are impossible to deny. But so are the risks of the collected data being misused or used for purposes that the data owner neither contemplated nor intended.

The sharing of enterprise data involves similar trade-offs between privacy and value, and balancing them requires the same level of care and forethought. The exploding volume of machine data from the Internet of Things will be used to generate high-value insights, but confidential information about companies and, potentially, employees will be at risk of misuse. With the rise of remote working, employee monitoring is blurring the boundary between personal and enterprise data.

B2B companies need a plan for dealing with IoT and other enterprise data privacy. What can they learn from the B2C experience with consumer data as they consider their own trade-offs between protecting proprietary information and capturing value from data sharing?

The Similarities Between Personal and Enterprise Data

The focus on personal-data rights reflects the inherent power imbalance between the individuals who share their data and the corporations that use that data to deliver services. Companies are expected to be responsible data stewards, and in some jurisdictions this responsibility is enshrined in regulations such as Europe's General Data Protection Regulation (GDPR) and the California Consumer Privacy Act. Enterprise data is actually quite similar to personal data and likewise demands good stewardship and attention to privacy issues.

https://doi.org/10.1515/9783110775112-010

Businesses use other companies' enterprise data in many of the same ways that they use consumers' personal data: to monitor compliance, understand behavior, make predictions, and gain insights into customers or competitors. Sharing data can unlock value by improving existing offerings and creating new ones. For example, connected car data can be used to create personalized insurance policies based on driver behavior or to launch whole new mobility-as-a-service models. Similarly, machine sensors can be used not only to customize maintenance and improve quality control but also to make new options for equipment use available through pay-per-use leasing models.

But both personal data and enterprise data can be sensitive. Just as individuals might not want to reveal their income, companies typically resist revealing non-public, often proprietary information that could be used by competitors.

To support new uses, new data and application marketplaces and ecosystems are taking shape. A whole industry has arisen to aggregate, process, and sell consumer data in order to better understand behavior, advertising effectiveness, infrastructure utilization, and public-health policy effectiveness, among many other applications. Similarly, IoT and other enterprise data is being aggregated and analyzed for new uses. For example, the maritime Automatic Identification System, originally intended to reduce collisions by tracking the identity and location of ships, is now the source of data for a wide range of other applications, including economic analysis, insurance, and oceanic research, among others.

This is all potentially good for the economy and for business, but there are challenges to address. One is that the data is constantly being collected in the background. Both personal IoT devices and connected equipment stream data to the cloud with limited awareness on the part of their users. Once this data is aggregated, it can become harder to protect the identity of the data source and other sensitive information. And as the data is further shared, it can easily be put to uses that go way beyond what the source of the data originally consented to.

Another issue is that enterprise data can contain personal information. For example, elevator traffic information in a commercial building, coupled with business address data, could be used to track the number or identity of customers or employees visiting a company location. Street sound sensors can identify a private home where a party is taking place, and machine operations data can track operator responsiveness. Even supposedly nonpersonal enterprise data can reveal personal information when combined with inferred-identity data.

An Evolving Consumer Data Landscape

Consent is the first line of defense when it comes to data privacy. But data from connected devices can be collected without much awareness or consent. Permissions are often buried deep in lengthy legal terms and conditions. Unclear consent agreements lead to a disconnect between the data that users think is being collected and how it is being used.[1] In many instances, users may not even be aware that they are sharing their data.

To encourage responsible data sharing, some companies have implemented best practices that consist of clear, transparent consent statements outlining what data is shared and how it is used. In Europe, the GDPR has directly addressed privacy risk by establishing the right to transparency, access, rectification, and erasure. A user may give permission to share limited data, such as whether a home is occupied, but not the identity of the resident. As data is transformed and aggregated downstream, these rights are supposed to follow the data, even as it flows through multiple intermediaries.

But personal-data ecosystems are complex and increasingly dominated by large players. The concentration of the smartphone market in many countries has led to two "superplatforms" – Apple and Google – that facilitate data capture and sharing, including GPS route guidance and location data. Intermediaries have emerged that buy, aggregate, and resell data to achieve scale in both data access and analytical capabilities. Against these powerful data players, individuals have little leverage or opportunity to shape the terms of data-sharing agreements.

Consumers are discerning about how much data to share and when. Though cautious, they are largely still willing to share their data for what they view as valuable use cases. In a 2019 survey by data aggregator Acxiom (now LiveRamp Holdings), more than 80% of respondents said they were concerned about the collection and use of personal data, but 58% were willing to "make trade-offs on a case-by-case basis as to whether the service or enhancement of service offered is worth the information requested." The business risk to companies that violate consumer trust can be high. Salesforce.com's 2019 "State of the Connected Customer" survey found that 72% of consumers would stop buying a company's products or using its services out of privacy concerns.

---

1 https://www.bcg.com/publications/2018/bridging-trust-gap-personal-data.

Lessons for Enterprise Data Sharing

B2B companies that hope to use IoT or other enterprise data in new or innovative ways should understand how evolving regulations and expectations around consumer data affect them. Rather than waiting for events to take their course, businesses can adopt best practices and self-regulatory processes to promote more robust enterprise data sharing. As companies look to balance risk and value, here are three important areas of focus.

Privacy and Intended Uses

Enterprises need to both define the rights of those that use the company's data and understand the company's rights with respect to its use of the data of others. A company that errs in either respect may incur financial and brand risk. For example, a company that makes data on factory equipment utilization available for industry aggregation purposes without proper protections could find equity traders extrapolating the company's financial performance from that data. It will be increasingly important to track the destination and uses of IoT data, especially as new use cases emerge that are very different from those that were originally envisioned. It is essential to make such information explicit not only in data-sharing agreements but also when buying equipment bundled with services that rely on the equipment's sensor data, since such equipment involves ongoing data-sharing and software-as-a-service arrangements.

Access control tools can enable permissioning in complex data-sharing setups. Just as consumers can choose to share only subsets of their personal data in order to access certain applications, enterprises may follow a similar approach with respect to IoT data, applying clear syndication rights and permissions. For example, smartphones today act as switchboards, enabling users to control which apps can access microphone, biometric, location, or camera data. Agricultural firm DKE-Data similarly enables farmers to control access to their machine and sensor data through a centralized interface, the Agrirouter. Multiple enterprise data platforms are emerging, such as Immuta and Talend, to help companies manage data rights, permissions, and syndications. As new data-sharing and aggregation platforms take shape, they will need to govern data access and use in ways that support data rights.

Value

Enterprises need to think creatively about the future value of their data. Complex ecosystems can enable data applications far from the data source, not only in the original industry but also in very different industries. Once potential use cases are identified, enterprises need to assess how critical the data is and whether substitutes are available today or will be in the future. Can the data be shared on a limited basis (such as in the form of metadata – which describes the data – or as a limited sample to invite innovation) while the company retains a financial option on the potential value of the data itself?

It will take significant effort to capture value from enterprise data. Given its heterogeneous nature, enterprise data requires more aggregation, transformation, processing, and analysis than consumer data in order to be turned into a product. In many cases, enterprises will need to invite complementary innovators to help unlock new solutions.

Sharing Options

For consumers, the core of a data-sharing decision is the trade-off between privacy and value. A similar assessment applies to enterprise IoT data. The level of data access will vary by use case and in each instance will sit at a different point on the spectrum between capturing value and protecting privacy.

Compared with individual consumers, companies have more opportunities to monetize their data and more resources and leverage to direct the ways in which that data is shared. Realizing these opportunities will require close collaboration between legal, procurement, digital, and business teams to determine the right level of data sharing in each use case. Questions to ask include the following:

- Does the data recipient need the entire raw data set, or would a metadata description or a sample subset suffice?
- For artificial intelligence applications that require large amounts of training data, could sharing synthetic data, or data that carries the statistical properties of real data but without its privacy risk, be a viable solution?
- What about allowing algorithms to train on your data without actually sharing it, an emerging AI technique called *federated learning*?

Thinking deliberately not just about *what* data to share but about *how* to share it can help balance data's innovation value against the potential disclosure risk to the enterprise.

B2B companies will eventually find myriad ways to generate value by sharing data with innovation partners. But assessing the trade-offs involved in each use case or set of permissions is at least as important for enterprises as it is for us as consumers. The experience of B2C companies – the early movers in data sharing – can help illuminate where both the potential and the pitfalls for B2B data sharers lie.

Section B: **Human-AI Collaboration**

Sam Ransbotham, Shervin Khodabandeh, David Kiron,
François Candelon, Michael Chu, Burt LaFountain
Chapter 11
Are You Making the Most of Your Relationship with AI?

Businesses everywhere are recognizing the power of AI to improve processes, meet customer needs, enter new spaces, and, above all, to gain sustainable competitive advantage. With this recognition has come an increased adoption of – and investment in – AI technologies. A global survey of more than 3,000 executives revealed that more than half of respondents are deploying AI: six out of ten have an AI strategy in 2020, up from four out of ten in 2018. AI solutions[1] are more prolific and easier to deploy than ever before, and companies around the globe are seizing on the opportunity to keep up with this exciting trend. Yet despite their efforts – to hire data scientists, develop algorithms, and optimize processes and decision making – most companies aren't seeing a significant return on their investments.

So, what allows a small number of companies to stand out from the crowd?

For them, AI isn't just a path to automation; it's an integral, strategic component of their businesses. To achieve significant financial benefits, companies must look beyond the initial, albeit fundamental, steps of AI adoption – of having the right data, technology, and talent in place, and organizing these elements around a corporate strategy. Currently, companies have only a 21% chance of achieving significant benefits with these fundamentals alone, though incorporating the ability to iterate on AI solutions with business users nearly doubles the number, to 39%. But it's the final stage of AI maturity, of successfully orchestrating the macro and micro interactions between humans and machines, that really unlocks value. The ability to learn as an organization – by bringing together human brains and the logic of machines – is what gives companies a 73% chance of reaping the financial benefits of AI implementation (Figure 11.1).

---

1 https://www.bcg.com/beyond-consulting/bcg-gamma/phosa-bcgs-ai-solution-for-continu ous-process-industries.

https://doi.org/10.1515/9783110775112-011

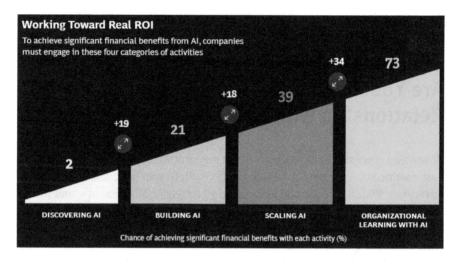

Figure 11.1: Successfully Orchestrating the Interactions Between Humans and Machines Unlocks Value.

A Symbiotic Relationship

These companies create opportunities for learning between humans and machines while acknowledging the strengths and weaknesses of each. They don't just teach machines what humans already know; they deploy whatever human-machine interaction the situation calls for, adapting as needed to changing context, circumstances, and scenarios. In short, these organizations recognize what AI can and cannot do – and what work is best left to humans (Figure 11.2). Like all strong organizations, they know where their different types of talent lie and, accordingly, where each is best suited to generate value.

Companies on the leading edge of AI adoption recognize that humans and machines must work together – and learn from one another. Within these businesses, AI technologies can learn autonomously and from human feedback, just as humans can learn from AI (Figure 11.3). But what matters most is that all three types of learning take place.

Figure 11.2: Deciding What AI Can Handle and What Is Best Left to Humans.

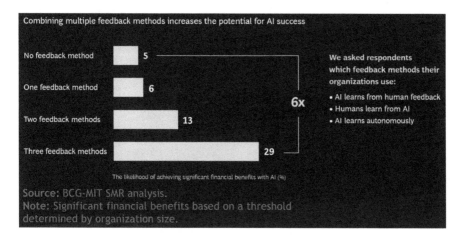

Figure 11.3: Building knowledge with better learning.

The Road Ahead is Long – and The Benefits are Worth It

Too many organizations build a strong AI foundation but fail to see the potential of what it can bring. Companies that have reaped the benefits have not succeeded simply because they've learned how to change in the era of AI. Instead, they've changed themselves to learn. They've committed to new organizational architectures, processes, behaviors, and attitudes. Such change can be uncomfortable and difficult to implement. It requires patience and flexibility, as well as the ability to adapt to new contexts and information. The good news? Companies that make significant changes see the biggest returns.

To embrace AI's full potential, companies must recognize that humans play an equally important role in the equation – and reshape themselves accordingly.

François Candelon, Michael Chu, Su Min Ha

Chapter 12
AI Won't Break Your Company's Culture – And It Might Even Boost Morale

For Pernod Ricard,[1] the $10 billion spirits and wine company whose flagship brands include Absolut, Chivas Regal, Jacob's Creek, and Malibu, accelerating its digital transformation is a priority.[2] Three years ago, when the French company started using artificial intelligence to drive sales, it braced itself for a revolt by its salespeople. But its fears proved to be unfounded. In fact, the salesforce embraced AI because the technology added to, rather than replaced, its experience and knowledge.

Pernod Ricard fostered trust in its algorithms by using business experts to design them, and by gathering extensive feedback from the first users. The company ensured that the reasoning behind the AI's decisions was communicated clearly to employees, and that its recommendations reinforced salespeople's pitches. Using AI has not only improved Pernod Ricard's performance, helping it optimize its advertising budget allocation and leading to increased revenues per salesperson, surprisingly, it has also changed the company's culture. "Our people are more confident, have greater clarity [about their roles], and morale is higher," points out Pierre-Yves Calloc'h, Pernod Ricard's chief digital officer.

Every CEO worries that culture will make or break their company's AI deployment,[3] but few realize that, conversely, AI can also transform organizational culture. When companies use the technology successfully, employees across the organization are able to perform more efficiently and collaborate more effectively. As a result, cultures change, altering employees' behaviors as well as their goals. The recent 2021 MIT SMR–BCG research report on AI,[4] based on a global survey of over 2,000 managers, identified – for the first time – a slew of cultural benefits that accrue because of AI, which we will focus on in this chapter.

Deploying AI, according to our study, changes one or more of the four dimensions of organizational culture, namely collective learning, collaboration, morale, and role clarity. In all, 58% of the companies we surveyed reported that the use of AI increased team efficiency and decision-making quality. And within

---

1 https://fortune.com/company/pernod-ricard.
2 https://www.pernod-ricard.com/en/our-group/our-strategy.
3 https://fortune.com/tag/artificial-intelligence/.
4 https://www.bcg.com/publications/2021/ai-benefits-company-culture.

https://doi.org/10.1515/9783110775112-012

that group, as many as 97% noticed an improvement in at least one of the culture-related parameters, while 51% of the sample registered improvements on all four dimensions.

Specifically, using AI results in the following:

More collective learning. Culture reflects the accumulated learning that one generation of employees passes on to the next. As many as 87% of the teams that improved their efficiency and decision quality by using AI also boosted their collective learning, according to the BCG-MIT survey.

In fact, AI influences both *what* teams learn and *how* learning occurs. For example, when the French B2B distribution company Rexel deployed a Next Best Offer tool that would recommend customized promotions, new salespeople rushed to use it, unlike the veterans. The latter were glad to have the AI-based tool, though, albeit for a different reason. New salespeople usually pester the veterans for ideas, but as the tool became better, they stopped doing so. That delighted the veterans, who could focus on their performance instead. Since the veterans were more eager to train the AI than to answer newcomers' questions, Rexel now uses the tool in the field as well as for vendor training. Instead of relying on a few employees' memories, Rexel's AI captures the current generation's knowledge and passes it on to the next generation whenever necessary.

Greater collaboration. AI done well leads to greater collaboration. According to the BCG-MIT survey, 59% of the respondents who were involved in AI projects reported better collaboration, while the number rose to 78% among those who saw improvements in efficiency and decision quality after using AI For instance, the airline KLM has started using AI to predict which checked-in passengers could miss their flights, sticking red tags on their luggage. That allowed baggage handlers to unload those bags quickly when necessary; pilots didn't have to delay departures as much; and flight attendants didn't have to pacify frustrated passengers. AI has helped align in real time KLM's cross-functional teams on the tarmac.

Clearer roles. AI helps executives and experts arrive at a new understanding of their roles. For example, pharmacists at US health care company Humana[5] used AI to improve their customer interactions. Using software that listened to pharmacists' conversations with patients, the AI picked up emotional cues, and then suggested what pharmacists could do to provide better customer experiences. That helped the pharmacists arrive at a better understanding of how to execute their roles, learning something new about themselves, customers, and handling customer calls. It's a standard result: Among the executives

---

5 https://fortune.com/company/humana.

who reported increases in efficiency and decision quality from AI, 65% reported greater clarity of roles.

Higher morale. As many as 79% of the survey respondents reported an increase in morale after the deployment of AI in their companies. For example, the Swedish fast-fashion retailer H&M Group experimented with AI to price products for end-of-season sales. It tested three processes: employee pricing, algorithm pricing, and employee-plus-algorithm pricing, with employees tweaking the algorithm's decisions. That last combination worked best, and employees welcomed the use of AI "Everybody loved it," recalls Arti Zeighami, former chief data and analytics officer at H&M. "They said, 'This makes me more precise. It helps me make better decisions. It makes my work more fun.'"

When AI helps a team become more effective, they naturally work better, with higher confidence and morale. But the very process of deploying AI can serve almost as therapy for the team. To build and work effectively with AI, employees have to question their core business principles and processes, asking themselves: What are we trying to achieve, how can we get there, and why is it important? That exercise sheds light on all the critical questions, bringing new levels of team effectiveness, what teams learn and how they learn, and how they work together. As a result, teams that use AI become more cohesive and stronger than they used to be.

Unsurprisingly, AI's effects on culture don't end at the team level – the benefits can extend to the entire organization. Using the technology helps companies explore new ways of creating value rather than merely improve existing processes. Those that do so are 2.7 times more likely to believe that their organization is better prepared to capture opportunities in adjacent industries than the latter.

Some companies use AI to reassess their strategic assumptions, using the technology to find performance drivers that they could not identify through experience or intuition. In fact, revising assumptions and measurements of performance is typical of organizations that have adopted AI; 64% of the companies that have integrated AI into their business processes say that doing so led to changes in performance indicators.

At the same time, adopting AI is not a magic carpet to a stronger culture; companies have to ensure that employees benefit tangibly from AI solutions before cultures will change. Moreover, the greater the process changes, the greater the improvements in morale. Companies that made many changes in business processes with AI were 1.5 times more likely to report an increase in morale compared to those that made no material changes despite adopting AI. Clearly, the more companies use AI, the more opportunities there will be for cultural benefit.

Understanding the relationship between AI and culture is important because the changes in the latter aren't just a marginal by-product; the cultural and the financial benefits from AI build on each other. According to our survey, companies that obtained substantial financial benefits from AI were 10 times more likely to change how they measure success than those who saw no benefits from it. They were also 20% more likely than the average to report that their organizations were better prepared to face competition.

Deploying AI at scale may not be easy, but CEOs would do well to remember that doing so will not only deliver financial benefits but also create high-performance cultures. And that's a claim few other technologies can make.

François Candelon, Su Min Ha, Colleen McDonald

Chapter 13
AI Could Make Your Company More Productive – But Not If It Makes Your People Less Happy

Artificial intelligence is all about productivity, right? AI-based software programs, such as Hubstaff, record keyboard strokes, mouse movements, and the websites employees visit when they work. Time Doctor uses webcams to shoot videos and pictures of users' screens at periodic intervals to check whether employees are at their computers. Isaak monitors employee interactions, combining its data with personnel records to identify the employees that are most collaborative. And Enable measures the time employees take to complete tasks, suggests ways they can speed up, and assigns productivity scores. Managers can use the grades to identify employees who are worth retaining – and those who aren't.

Whatever you may privately feel about the technology, AI is here to stay. But have business leaders developed the right attitude to productivity in the AI Age?

Machine productivity, measured by the quantitative output produced every minute, hour, or day, can be mechanically monitored and managed. But we humans aren't exactly machines. Science shows that we work best when we mix work with breaks,[1] and that we're most motivated when we enjoy ownership and independence.[2] These "human" factors demand a nuanced perspective on productivity that digital technologies may not yet possess. Still, shunning the technology isn't the answer; used in the right way, AI can benefit both employees and businesses, as a recent BCG–MIT research project[3] has shown. The key is for companies to ensure that the productivity of both humans and AI rises as they work together, and that they bring out the best in each other.

Sadly, companies, especially those that have started using AI in the workplace, tend to focus only on the technology and almost forget about the human aspects while trying to optimize productivity. CEOs, we believe, must tackle four challenges to get the most out of combining employees and AI: excessive oversight, isolation, leftover tasks, and dependence.

---

1 https://qz.com/work/1561830/why-the-eight-hour-workday-doesnt-work/.
2 https://qz.com/676144/why-its-your-call-is-the-best-thing-you-can-say-to-keep-employees-happy/.
3 https://www.bcg.com/publications/2021/ai-benefits-company-culture.

https://doi.org/10.1515/9783110775112-013

Excessive Oversight

Companies can use digital technologies to collect data on (almost) everything that their employees do. Doing so usually leads to executives micromanaging employees so much that the process often borders on the invasion of their privacy. Besides, using AI to ensure that people are working every second will increase the productivity only of those who need constant supervision. It will never inspire creativity and innovation – the capabilities that differentiate humans from machines.

One antidote may be to use AI for employee self-development rather than monitoring them. Microsoft's Viva Insights,[4] for instance, is an AI-powered platform that gathers data on parameters such as the time employees spend checking email and interacting with colleagues, and alerting them when they need to take breaks. One feature, Reflection, privately tells employees how they've been feeling; another, Send Praise, makes it easy to express appreciation to coworkers; and Virtual Commute reminds employees when they should start wrapping up as the day ends. Viva brings insights and communications to where employees work, changing the nature of education into a real-time process.

Managers can only track aggregate figures, such as the percentage of employees who spent over a third of their time in long meetings (over an hour) and large meetings (over eight people); those with less than 20 hours of focus time a week; and people who spend less than an hour a week in one-on-one sessions with managers. Thus, Viva helps managers coach employees, a focus that makes the latter more open to using the AI-based software.

Isolation

Relationships at work increase employee motivation, well-being, and productivity. According to a recent Gallup study,[5] people who have at least one close friend at work are seven times as likely to be engaged, produce higher quality work, and enjoy greater well-being than those who have none. Still, as employees learn to work with AI, they will spend less time with coworkers. For instance, autonomous factories will require employees to work in isolation for prolonged periods; AI could replace interactions between team leaders and members; and

---

4 https://www.microsoft.com/en-us/microsoft-viva/insights.
5 https://news.gallup.com/businessjournal/127043/friends-social-wellbeing.aspx.

algorithms may even execute layoff decisions – as apparently already happens in Amazon's warehouses.[6]

That's why companies must take care to create episodes of employee interdependence and moments of interaction. For instance, Humanyze, a people analytics firm, found while working with a US bank that those of its call centers whose employees had frequent social interactions reported higher productivity and greater retention. It therefore suggested that the bank synchronize the breaks in all the call centers to create more opportunities for interaction. One year after the bank did so, its call centers reported[7] a 23% increase in productivity and a 28% increase in retention.

Leftover Tasks

As the use of automation increases, employees will often have to take on residual tasks that can be physically or mentally demanding. Some Amazon[8] workers complain that they have to stand in one spot for hours, picking up objects from conveyor belts and placing them on shelves (grabbing is tough for the robots in the warehouse). The task is, evidently, punishing; between 2017 and 2019, Amazon's warehouses reported 8.9 injuries per 100 employees[9] – 40% of which were related to repetitive motions – which is over three times as high as the US average of 2.8 injuries per 100 employees. Similarly, when AI in call centers takes care of simple problems – "I forgot my login" – employees are left to deal with back-to-back calls from the most unhappy and angriest customers. That adds more stress to demanding and underpaying jobs.

Relying on employees to only do what machines can't is neither productive nor sustainable; employee turnover will inevitably increase. Moreover, business will find it difficult to fill those bad jobs and expensive to constantly train new people for them. Companies should therefore keep both eyes focused on the human dimension as they deploy AI. Amazon itself has doubled down on workplace wellness,[10] launching a fresh initiative as part of a $300 million safety

---

6 https://www.theverge.com/2019/4/25/18516004/amazon-warehouse-fulfillment-centers-productivity-firing-terminations.

7 https://humanyze.com/case-studies-major-us-bank/.

8 https://fortune.com/company/amazon-com.

9 https://www.cnbc.com/2021/05/17/relentless-amazon-has-new-plan-to-cut-worker-injuries-by-50percent-.html.

10 https://www.cnbc.com/2021/05/17/relentless-amazon-has-new-plan-to-cut-worker-injuries-by-50percent-.html.

program it kicked off in 2019. There's room for improvement, but injury rates in Amazon's warehouses did fall last year.

Dependence

As AI becomes better, companies run the risk of becoming overly dependent on the technology. One of our clients found that the accuracy of its algorithm's predictions was apparently close to 100%, but its data scientists pointed out that it was unlikely – the accuracy could be around 85% at most. An investigation revealed that employees were assuming that the AI's predictions were correct without even checking if they were. Such overreliance can cause problems both when the algorithm doesn't work and, worse, when no one realizes that it isn't accurate.

To avoid depending too much on AI, companies should train employees to manually execute business processes even if they've been automated. It's no different from training pilots, who must know how to take off, fly, and land a plane in case its autopilot system fails. Algorithms may be sophisticated, but it's still necessary to build human oversight into the critical parts of business processes. And organizations should create systems so that employees can raise red flags about AI without worrying that they will be punished in case they've erred.

***

As AI's use in business becomes more prevalent, CEOs must shift their attention in the year ahead to ensure that both the technology and their people deliver better results – AI + Human = Productivity, as the equation goes. Leaders should focus on their people, motivate them, facilitate their development – and inspire them, so they stay involved and innovative. AI may be a powerful technology, but nothing will get better by simply adding AI to anything.

Section C: **Responsible AI and the Social License to Operate**

François Candelon, Rodolphe Charme di Carlo, Steven D. Mills
Chapter 14
AI-at-Scale Hinges on Gaining a "Social License"

In January 2020, an unknown American facial recognition software company, Clearview AI, was thrust into the limelight. It had quietly flown under the radar until *The New York Times*[1] reported that businesses, law enforcement agencies, universities, and individuals had been purchasing its sophisticated facial recognition software, whose algorithm could match human faces to a database of over 3 billion images the company had collected from the internet. The article renewed the global debate about the use of AI-based facial recognition technology by governments and law enforcement agencies.

Many people called for a ban on the use of the Clearview AI technology because the startup had created its database by mining social media websites and the internet for photographs but hadn't obtained permission to index individuals' faces. Twitter almost immediately sent the company a cease-and-delete letter, and YouTube and Facebook followed suit. When the COVID-19 pandemic erupted in March 2020, Clearview tried to pitch its technology for use in contact tracing in an effort to regain its credibility and gain social acceptance. Although Clearview's AI technology could have helped tackle the crisis, the manner in which the company had gathered data and created its data sets created a social firestorm that discouraged its use.

In business, as in life, being responsible is necessary but far from sufficient to build trust. As exemplified by the controversies around some corporations' AI applications – such as Amazon,[2] which had to terminate its experiment with a resume-screening algorithm, and Microsoft,[3] whose AI-based chatbot was a public relations disaster – society will not agree to the use of AI applications, however responsibly they may have been developed, if they haven't *a priori* earned people's trust.

Rational people have a variety of concerns about AI, including the algorithmic institutionalization of income, gender, racial, and geographic prejudices; privacy

1 https://www.nytimes.com/2020/01/18/technology/clearview-privacy-facial-recognition.html.

2 https://www.reuters.com/article/us-amazon-com-jobs-automation-insight/amazon-scraps-secret-ai-recruiting-tool-that-showed-bias-against-women-idUSKCN1MK08G.

3 https://www.theverge.com/2016/3/24/11297050/tay-microsoft-chatbot-racist.

https://doi.org/10.1515/9783110775112-014

concerns; and political issues. Indeed, Georgetown University's Center for Security and Emerging Technology and the Partnership on AI last year launched the AI Incident Database[4] to record cases in which intelligent systems have caused safety, fairness, or other real-world problems; as of July, it listed 1,200 publicly reported cases of such AI failures from the past three years. That's why companies are struggling to come to terms with the gulf between what they understand to be their legal rights to use AI and their social right, which they don't possess by default.

Why Responsible AI Isn't Enough

Adhering to the concepts of responsible AI enables companies to develop AI technology that works for the good; it forces business to go beyond algorithmic fairness and bias to identify the technology's potential effects on safety and privacy. However, following the doctrine of responsible AI has proven to be insufficient for two main reasons. First, it embodies a technology-based approach, with the focus squarely on the technical challenge of building goodness and fairness into algorithms. However, it's impossible to eliminate bias from AI unless all humans become good, fair, and unbiased – and that isn't likely to happen anytime soon.

Second, without formal regulations to follow, the articulation of each organization's principles, as well as its adherence to them, has been left to the very data scientists and software developers who write algorithms. Thus, the principles naturally vary from company to company, and, inside organizations, by business and even function, which is hardly ideal. The issue has been further complicated by the variance among the multiple responsible AI guidelines and principles proposed by different organizations and companies.

Underlying the issue is the reality that while being trusted and being responsible may be related, they are distinct from each other. Responsibility may foster trust, but it can never be a substitute for it.

Before businesses can obtain society's explicit approval to use AI applications at scale, two things need to happen. First, public institutions must enact laws and regulations, and companies must face penalties for not abiding by them. Second, businesses must adopt a human-focused approach that fosters trust among all their stakeholders – employees, executives, suppliers, shareholders, communities, civil society, and government – in the AI applications

---

4 https://www.partnershiponai.org/aiincidentdatabase/.

they develop. Thus, companies must gain what could be thought of as a social license for AI applications.

The Foundations of Trust

Stakeholders' trust in AI applications stem from three sources (see Figure 14.1):
1. **Social contracts.** Stakeholders must accept that companies that develop AI applications can be trusted with their use as well as with the acquisition of real-time data to feed their algorithms. This especially holds true in cases where the algorithms can act independently of supervision and may have an impact on human lives. That's one reason why countries have been slow to approve the unrestricted use of self-driving automobiles.
2. **Benefits.** Businesses' perception that the advantages of using AI are greater than the costs of doing so must be widely shared by other stakeholders. It must be possible to determine the tangible and intangible trade-offs at the individual, company, and societal levels by weighing the benefits of AI-delivered outcomes – such as increased health, convenience, and comfort, in the case of health care – against the potential downsides, such as reduced security, privacy, or safety. Society's verdict may not always favor the use of an application, and businesses should be prepared for that.
3. **Responsibility.** If companies are to be answerable to society, they must be able to justify how their AI algorithms work. Businesses should be as open as they can about the algorithms they design and, whenever necessary, be able to explain the manner in which they arrive at their decisions. AI will be deemed fair only if the outcomes generated by the technology don't vary based on demographic factors or contextual changes. For example, a company that uses an AI-based recruitment system must be able to demonstrate that all of the candidates who provided the same or similar responses to a question posed by the machine on different days received the same rating or score.

Winning Trust Through Dialogue

To develop society's trust, companies must initiate discussions with *all* of their stakeholders to bring out the reactions, motivations, positions, and objections of different groups of people. These conversations will allow companies to

Winning a social license to deploy AI will require organizations to adhere to the principles of responsible AI design; ensure that all stakeholders perceive the benefits of using AI as greater than the costs; and demonstrate that they can be trusted and will be accountable.

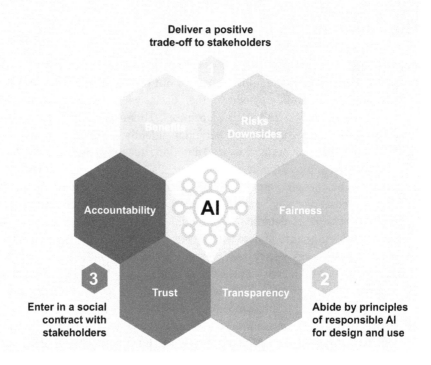

Figure 14.1: The Three Sources of Stakeholders' Trust in AI Applications.

develop a shared understanding with stakeholders about each AI application and the guardrails that must fence its deployment.

Companies can work to gain stakeholders' trust in AI by taking four steps:

1. **Identify stakeholders.** The number of stakeholders whose trust will be required will vary according to the problem the AI system is trying to tackle. For instance, when German delivery company DHL wished to install an AI-based pallet-sorting system two years ago, it had to worry only about the reactions of employees, trade unions, and shareholders. In contrast, Waymo and Tesla must work with a large number of stakeholders – automobile owners and drivers (consumers); city, state, and central governments (regulators); and civil society (critics and advocates) – to obtain a social license for self-driving technologies.

2. **Be transparent.** Whether it is the assumptions underlying their algorithms or the impact of AI on employees, transparency alone will go a long way toward allowing businesses to proceed with the use of AI applications.

Many companies haven't developed the expertise to explain how their algorithms work without giving away proprietary information. They must partner with the major AI players to figure out how to do so. For example, scientists are creating *self-explainable AI*[5] that can provide a decision as well as a supporting explanation, without sacrificing the accuracy of the former. In the same way, *causal AI* identifies the factors in an algorithm that lead to particular outcomes and then tests what will change them. Participating in AI ecosystems or partnering with government initiatives, such as the US Defense Advanced Research Projects Agency's Explainable Artificial Intelligence project,[6] can give businesses access to tools and techniques for fostering transparency.

Companies must be open internally about the implications for their workforce when they implement AI. They must identify the gaps as well as the surpluses in the workforce[7] that will be created by the use of AI and develop forecasts for the job functions that will be most significantly affected by an application's rollout. Businesses must upskill and reskill affected employees, whenever possible, in order to fill new positions – while being transparent about the effects on compensation. Not all jobs created as a result of AI will necessarily pay better than those rendered obsolete by AI.

3. **Manage risk.** Companies must learn to mitigate AI-related risks by carefully mapping and evaluating their severity and probability – as well as the context, such as the regulatory environment. Managing AI-related risks doesn't differ much from tackling other kinds of risk; chief risk officers can determine the levels of legal, financial, reputational, and physical risk they're willing to take.

However systematic risks are assessed, companies must institutionalize human oversight over AI. They must ensure that the AI system learns to flag exceptions that it cannot process and recommend human over-the-loop interventions to deal with them. In March 2020, for example, the AI-based cybersecurity mechanisms of one of Britain's premier online grocery stores suddenly shut down its website because it had confused the COVID-19-related surge in demand with a distributed denial-of-service attack. If the retailer had created a way for human decision makers to monitor and override the system's knee-jerk

5 https://arxiv.org/abs/2002.05149.

6 https://www.darpa.mil/program/explainable-artificial-intelligence.

7 https://www.bcg.com/publications/2019/decoding-digital-talent.

response, it would have generated more revenue rather than irritating customers that day.

4. **Communicate and educate.** Companies have to explain all the possible benefits of their AI applications as well as all the potential downsides. They shouldn't shy away from describing the risks while explaining how it will tackle them. Google, for example, shares an organization wide commitment to ensuring the safe, fair, and unbiased use of AI by publishing and periodically updating its principles for responsible AI.[8] It serves as a public reference for anyone who wants to hold the company accountable for complying with its own rules.

Business would do well to help governments at all levels understand the technology and its impact. Regulators find it difficult to keep pace with technology and should welcome the help of business leaders in developing AI-related policies. Close engagement with governments will help companies proactively develop AI technology that aligns with the direction of future laws and regulations; meanwhile, regulators could help accelerate the pace at which AI earns social approval.

Currently, businesses planning to deploy AI are most concerned with obtaining an economic license to do so – that is, gaining support from shareholders and executives – and a legal license, in the form of regulatory permits and compliance with statutory obligations. But only when companies are able to earn a social license, winning the trust of employees, customers, and society at large, will they have what is required for the sustained use of AI at scale.

---

8 https://ai.google/principles/.

François Candelon, Theodoros Evgeniou
Chapter 15
With AI, Business Leaders Must Prioritize Safety Over Speed

Two years ago, before Apple's launch of the Apple Card,[1] there was much discussion about how the no-fee credit card would enable the tech giant to storm into the financial services business. However, when people discuss the Apple Card today, it's in part because of the glitches in Apple's artificial intelligence[2] algorithms that determine wannabe cardholders' credit limits.

In November 2019, a Dane tweeted[3] that while his wife and he had both applied for the Apple Card with the same financial information, he was awarded a credit limit 20 times higher than that of his wife – even though, as he admitted, his wife had a higher credit score. Adding fuel to the fire, Apple's cofounder, Steve Wozniak, claimed that the same thing had happened to his wife. The card had been launched in August 2019, and it was estimated that there were 3.1 million Apple Card credit card holders in the US at the beginning of 2020, so this issue may well have affected tens of thousands of women. A spate of complaints resulted in a New York Department of Financial Services investigation, which recently cleared Apple[4] of gender-based discrimination, but only after the digital giant quietly raised wives' credit limits to match those of their husbands.

As business sets about deploying AI at scale, the focus is increasingly shifting from the use of the technology to create and capture value to the inherent risks that AI-based systems entail. Watchdog bodies such as the Artificial Intelligence Incident Database[5] have already documented hundreds of cases of AI-related complaints, ranging from the questionable scoring of students' exams[6] to the inappropriate use of algorithms in recruiting[7] and the differential treatment of patients by health care systems.[8] As a result, companies will soon have

---

1 https://fortune.com/company/apple.
2 https://fortune.com/2019/11/13/apple-card-bias-women-goldman-sachs/.
3 https://twitter.com/dhh/status/1192540900393705474.
4 https://www.dfs.ny.gov/reports_and_publications/press_releases/pr202103231.
5 https://www.partnershiponai.org/aiincidentdatabase/?utm_campaign=Your%20guide%20to%20AI&utm_medium=email&utm_source=Revue%20newsletter.
6 https://www.wired.com/story/algorithm-set-students-grades-altered-futures/.
7 https://www.wired.com/story/job-screening-service-halts-facial-analysis-applicants/.
8 https://science.sciencemag.org/content/366/6464/447.

https://doi.org/10.1515/9783110775112-015

to comply with regulations in several countries that aim to ensure that AI-based systems are trustworthy, safe, robust, and fair. Once again, the European Union is leading the way, outlining a framework last year in its *White Paper on Artificial Intelligence: A European Approach to Excellence and Trust,*[9] as well as its proposal for a legal framework in April 2021.

Companies must learn to tackle AI risks not only because it will be a regulatory requirement, but because stakeholders will expect them to do so. As many as 60% of executives reported that their organizations decided against working with AI service providers last year due to responsibility-related concerns, according to a recent Economist Intelligence Unit study.[10] To effectively manage AI, business must grasp the implications of regulations and social expectations on its use even while keeping in mind the technology's unique characteristics, which we've discussed at length in our recent *Harvard Business Review* article.[11] Indeed, figuring out how to balance the rewards from using AI with the risks could well prove to be a new, and sustainable, source of competitive advantage.

To Learn, or Not to Learn?

At the outset, consider AI's much-vaunted ability to continuously become better by learning from the data it studies – a characteristic that makes AI a unique technology. The virtuous cycle can lead to AI behavior that cannot always be anticipated, as the example of Microsoft's chatbot, Tay, showed[12] in 2016, or to outcomes that may raise concerns of fairness, as Amazon's use of AI to screen résumés[13] vividly demonstrated. An AI system can make one decision one day, and, learning from the data it is subsequently fed, could arrive at a vastly different decision the very next day. That's why US regulators, such as the Food and Drug Administration, approve only algorithms that don't evolve during their use.

Similarly, companies will need to decide whether or not to allow their AI systems to learn in real time. Not allowing continuous learning will, sadly, result in companies having to forgo one of the key benefits of AI, namely its ability to perform better over time, in some cases. In others, business will need to balance the

---

9 https://ec.europa.eu/info/publications/white-paper-artificial-intelligence-european-approach-excellence-and-trust_en.

10 https://pages.eiu.com/rs/753-RIQ-438/images/EIUStayingAheadOfTheCurve.pdf.

11 https://hbr.org/2021/09/ai-regulation-is-coming.

12 https://www.theverge.com/2016/3/24/11297050/tay-microsoft-chatbot-racist.

13 https://www.businessinsider.com/amazon-built-ai-to-hire-people-discriminated-against-women-2018-10.

trade-offs between risk levels and algorithmic accuracy, which will be hampered if companies don't allow continuous learning.

Ever-evolving AI systems also generate operational complexities because the same AI-embedded product or service will work differently in each country. These operational challenges will be compounded by the subtle variations in regulations and social expectations in each nation. Companies will have to train their AI using local data and manage them according to local regulations. That is bound to limit AI's ability to scale.

In addition, companies will have to treat their AI as a portfolio of applications that needs careful management. They will have to develop sentinel processes to monitor the portfolio, continuously ensuring its fair, safe, and robust functioning. Organizations will have to frequently test the output of AI systems, which will add to costs. For example, a 2017 New York City law[14] mandated the creation of a task force to provide recommendations on how information on automated decision systems should be shared with the public, and how public agencies should address instances where people could be harmed by automated decision systems.

Taking Responsibility for AI's Decisions

Another key differentiator is AI's ability to make complex decisions, such as which ads to serve up online to whom or whether to grant facial recognition–based access. Responsibility comes hand-in-hand with the ability to make decisions. So far, companies and other organizations acting according to the principles of Responsible AI[15] have focused on ensuring that AI-based decisions treat all stakeholders – consumers, employees, shareholders, stakeholders – fairly. If AI algorithms treat people unfairly, companies will face legal and reputational risks, as Apple did. They need to understand the possible impact that their algorithms can have on humans, and even choose not to use AI in some contexts. These concerns will be exacerbated as AI systems scale; an algorithm may be fair, on average, but may still be unfair in specific geographical contexts because local consumer behavior and attitudes may not correspond to the average, and thus may not be reflected in the algorithm's training.

---

14 https://foundationsoflawandsociety.wordpress.com/2020/12/08/nyc-local-law-49-a-first-attempt-at-regulating-algorithms/.
15 https://www.bcg.com/publications/2020/six-steps-for-socially-responsible-artificial-intelligence.

Companies have no option but to develop processes, roles, and functions to ensure that AI systems are fair and responsible. Some, like the Federal Home Loan Mortgage Corporation (Freddie Mac), have already appointed AI ethics officers and set up AI governance structures and processes – such as traceability protocols and diversity training – to tackle this challenge, which are small steps in the right direction. In addition, the pioneers are setting up auditing processes and developing monitoring tools to ensure the fair functioning of AI systems.

Accountability requires companies to explain why their algorithms make decisions the way they do. This idea of "explainability" will force companies to make trade-offs. Easier-to-explain algorithms are usually less accurate than so-called black box algorithms, so if companies use only the former, it will limit the AI's abilities and quality. Because executives will have to make trade-offs between explainability and accuracy, it's bound to create an unequal playing field across the globe since market regulations and social expectations will differ across nations.

By way of illustration: Ant Financial combines thousands of inputs from data sources in the Alibaba ecosystem to develop credit ratings for borrowers in China. The process makes it difficult for anyone, even regulators,[16] to understand how the algorithms make decisions. While Alibaba's systems allow the company to approve loans within minutes, it may not be able to use the same system outside China, especially in economies with regulations and expectations that demand a higher degree of explainability. Consequently, AI regulations will limit the markets that AI-driven companies can target, which has major strategy implications. In fact, a few companies, such as game developer Uber Entertainment,[17] chose to stay away from the EU after the enactment of the General Data Privacy Regulation in 2019.

As more governments unveil rules about the use of AI, companies will need to consider some key questions before deploying AI They must ask themselves:

- To what extent should we differentiate our product or service offering to follow local differences in AI regulations and market expectations?
- Should we still serve all these markets worldwide after accounting for the new regulatory landscape?
- If decentralizing AI operations is essential, should we set up a central organization to lead, or at least connect, the sharing of data, algorithms, insights, and best practices?

---

16 https://fortune.com/2021/08/16/big-tech-regulations-europe-explainer/.
17 https://money.cnn.com/2018/05/11/technology/gdpr-tech-companies-losers/index.html.

- Given AI regulations and market expectations, what are the new roles and organizational capabilities that we will need to ensure that our strategy and execution are aligned? How will we hire, or reskill, talent to acquire these capabilities?
- Is our strategy horizon appropriate to combine the short-run responses to a constantly changing technology and regulatory environment with our long-term AI vision?

As the use of AI in companies' internal and external processes becomes more pervasive, and the expectations of stakeholders about fair, safe, and trustworthy AI rise, companies are bound to run headlong into man vs. machine clashes. The sooner CEOs come to grips with the value-risk trade-offs of using AI-driven systems, the better they will be able to cope with both regulations and expectations in an AI-driven world.

Steven D. Mills, Daniel Lim

Chapter 16
This Is Why We Need to Talk About Responsible AI

Bias in AI and other negative consequences of the technology have become common media fodder. The impression that media coverage gives is that only a few companies are taking steps to ensure the AI systems they develop aren't inadvertently harming users or society. But results from an IDC survey[1] show that many companies are moving toward *Responsible AI*. Nearly 50% of organizations reported having a formalized framework to encourage considerations of ethics, bias and trust.

But why are so few companies pulling back the curtain to share how they are approaching this emerging focus? The silence is puzzling given the commitment to the responsible use of technology these investments signal.

Work in Progress

Responsible AI is still a relatively new field that has rapidly developed over the past two years, with one of the first public guidelines[2] for implementing Responsible AI in 2018. Yet only a few companies are publicly discussing their ongoing work in this area in a substantive, transparent, and proactive way. Many other companies, however, seem to fear negative consequences (like reputational risk) of sharing their vulnerabilities. Some companies are also waiting for a "finished product," wanting to be able to point to tangible, positive outcomes before they are ready to reveal their work. They feel it is important to convey that they have a robust solution with all the answers to all the problems relevant to their business.

We've also seen that willingness to be transparent varies by industry. For example, an enterprise software company that speaks regularly about bug fixes

---

1 https://blogs.idc.com/2021/02/19/why-organizations-should-care-about-responsible-ai-digital-ethics/.
2 https://urldefense.proofpoint.com/v2/url?u=https-3A__blogs.microsoft.com_blog_2018_11_14_microsoft-2Dintroduces-2Dguidelines-2Dfor-2Ddeveloping-2Dresponsible-2Dconversational-2Dai_&d=DwMGaQ&c=VWART3hH1Kkv_uOe9JqhCg&r=pDnL0fGd7OlAEnRiWGOGcfLwe4VFTe24AUelGy.

https://doi.org/10.1515/9783110775112-016

and new versioning may find Responsible AI to be a natural next step in their business. However, a company that monetizes data may worry that creating this kind of transparency will unearth greater stakeholders concern about the business model itself.

Through our conversations with companies, we've seen no one has conquered Responsible AI, and everyone is approaching it from a different angle. And largely, there is more to gain from sharing and learning than continuing to work toward perfection in silos.

All Risk and No Reward?

With so many news stories about AI gone wrong,[3] it's easy to keep the strategies under wraps. But it's important to understand the reward of sharing lessons with communities.

First, talking openly about efforts to improve algorithms will build trust with customers – and trust is one of the greatest competitive advantages a company can have.[4] Furthermore, as companies like Apple have proven,[5] embracing a customer-centric approach that incorporates feedback loops helps build better products. Making Responsible AI part of stakeholder feedback will not only help avoid reputational damage but will ultimately increase customer engagement. Finally, the data science profession is still in its early stages of maturity. Models and frameworks that incorporate ethics into the problem solving process, such as the one published by researchers at the University of Virginia,[6] are just beginning to emerge.

As a result, Responsible AI practices such as societal impact assessments and bias detection are just starting to make their way into the methodologies of data scientists. By discussing their challenges with their peers in other companies, data scientists and developers can create community, solve problems and, in the end, improve the entire AI field.

As champions of Responsible AI, we urge companies to lean into Responsible AI, engaging with peers and experts to share not only the wins, but also the challenges. Companies must work together to advance the industry and build technology for the good of all.

---

3 https://medium.com/syncedreview/2019-in-review-10-ai-failures-317b46155350.
4 https://www.bcg.com/publications/2018/bridging-trust-gap-personal-data.
5 https://hbr.org/2020/01/why-the-best-developers-keep-customers-front-of-mind.
6 https://hdsr.mitpress.mit.edu/pub/hnptx6lq.

Five Ways to Join The Responsible AI Discussion

We've taken our conversations with corporate executives and through our participation in the World Economic Forum Responsible Use of Technology[7] project community, and distilled our learning into five areas where companies can help build transparency into their Responsible AI initiatives (Figure 16.1).

Image: World Economic Forum

Figure 16.1: Five Ways to Build Responsible AI Initiatives.

1. **Create and engage in safe spaces to learn.** Closed forums such as the World Economic Forum Responsible Use of Technology[8] project provide a safe, achievable step toward transparency – a place for companies to speak openly in a risk-free, peer-to-peer setting. Interactions with other companies can accelerate knowledge sharing on Responsible AI practices, and build confidence in your own efforts.
2. **Engage your customers and community.** Customer engagement and feedback builds stronger products. Adding Responsible AI to these dialogues is a great way to engage with customers in a low-risk, comfortable environment.
3. **Be deliberate.** You don't need to go from "zero to press release." Give your program time to develop: Begin with dialogue in closed forums, speak with your employees, maybe author a blog post, then expand from there. The important thing is to take steps toward transparency. The size of the steps

---

7 https://www.weforum.org/projects/responsible-use-of-technology.
8 https://www.weforum.org/projects/responsible-use-of-technology.

is less important. Taking this progressive approach will also help you find your voice.

4. **Diversity matters.** Engaging with stakeholders from diverse backgrounds is an essential step in the process of improving Responsible AI. Actively listening to and addressing the concerns of people with different perspectives throughout the design, deployment, and adoption of AI systems can help identify and mitigate unintended consequences. This approach may also lead to the creation of better products that serve a larger market.

5. **Set the right tone.** Cultural change starts at the top. Senior executives need to set a tone of openness and transparency to create comfort sharing vulnerabilities and learnings. Ultimately, this will ease organizational resistance to engaging in public dialogue about Responsible AI.

We are still in the early stages of Responsible AI, but we can make rapid progress if we work together to share successes, learning, and challenges.

Steven D. Mills, Elias Baltassis, Maximiliano Santinelli,
Cathy Carlisi, Sylvain Duranton, Andrea Gallego

Chapter 17
Six Steps to Bridge the Responsible AI Gap

As artificial intelligence[1] assumes a more central role in countless aspects of business and society, so has the need for ensuring its responsible use. AI has dramatically improved financial performance, employee experience, and product and service quality for millions of customers and citizens, but it has also inflicted harm. AI systems have offered lower credit card limits to women than men despite similar financial profiles. Digital ads have demonstrated racial bias in housing and mortgage offers. Users have tricked chatbots into making offensive and racist comments. Algorithms have produced inaccurate diagnoses and recommendations for cancer treatments.

To counter such AI fails, companies have recognized the need to develop and operate AI systems that work in the service of good while achieving transformative business impact[2] – thinking beyond bare-bones algorithmic fairness and bias in order to identify potential second- and third-order effects on safety, privacy, and society at large. These are all elements of what has become known as Responsible AI.

Companies know they need to develop this capability, and many have already created Responsible AI principles to guide their actions. The big challenge lies in execution. Companies often don't recognize, or know how to bridge, the gulf between principles and tangible actions – what we call crossing the "Responsible AI Gap." To help cross the divide, we have distilled our learnings from engagements with multiple organizations into six basic steps that companies can follow.

The Upside of Responsible AI

Concern is growing both inside and outside boardrooms about the ethical risks associated with AI systems. A survey conducted by the Center for the Governance

---

1 https://www.bcg.com/capabilities/digital-technology-data/artificial-intelligence.
2 https://medium.com/bcggamma/the-challenge-of-defining-responsible-ai-858120fdbaaa.

https://doi.org/10.1515/9783110775112-017

of AI at the University of Oxford showed that 82% of respondents[3] believe that AI should be carefully managed. Two-thirds of internet users[4] surveyed by the Brookings Institution feel that companies should have an AI code of ethics and review board.

Much of this concern has arisen from failures of AI systems that have received widespread media attention. Executives have begun to understand the risks that poorly designed AI systems can create – from costly litigation to financial losses. The reputational damage and employee disengagement that result from public AI lapses can have far-reaching effects.

But companies should not view Responsible AI simply as a risk-avoidance mechanism. Doing so misses the upside potential that companies can realize by pursuing it. In addition to representing an authentic and ethical "True North" to guide initiatives, Responsible AI can generate financial rewards that justify the investment.

A Stronger Bottom Line

Companies that practice Responsible AI – and let their clients and users know they do so – have the potential to increase market share and long-term profitability. Responsible AI can be used to build high-performing systems with more reliable and explainable outcomes. When based on the authentic and ethical strengths of an organization, these outcomes help build greater trust, improve customer loyalty, and ultimately boost revenues. Major companies such as Salesforce, Microsoft, and Google have publicized the robust steps they have taken to implement Responsible AI. And for good reason: people weigh ethics three times more heavily than competence[5] when assessing a company's trustworthiness, according to Edelman research. Lack of trust carries a heavy financial cost. In the US, BCG research shows that companies lost one-third of revenue from affected customers[6] in the year following a data misuse incident.

---

3 https://governanceai.github.io/US-Public-Opinion-Report-Jan-2019/us_public_opinion_re port_jan_2019.pdf.
4 https://www.brookings.edu/research/how-to-address-ai-ethical-dilemmas/.
5 https://www.edelman.com/sites/g/files/aatuss191/files/2020-01/2020%20Edelman%20Trust% 20Barometer%20Global%20Report.pdf.
6 https://www.bcg.com/publications/2018/bridging-trust-gap-personal-data.

Brand Differentiation

Increasingly, companies have grown more focused on staying true to their purpose[7] and their foundational principles. In addition, customers are increasingly making choices to do business with companies whose demonstrated values are aligned with their own. Companies that deliver what BCG calls total societal impact (TSI)[8] – the aggregate of their impact on society – boast higher margins and valuations. Organizations must make sure that their AI initiatives are aligned with what they truly value and the positive impact they seek to make through their purpose. The benefit of focusing strictly on compliance pales in comparison with the value gained from strengthening connections to customers and employees in an increasingly competitive business environment.

Improved Recruiting and Retention

Responsible AI helps attract the elite digital talent that is critical to the success of firms[9] worldwide. In the UK, one in six AI workers has quit his or her job rather than having to play a role in the development of potentially harmful products. That's more than three times the rate of the technology sector as a whole,[10] according to research from Doteveryone. In addition to inspiring the employees who build and deploy AI, implementing AI systems in a responsible manner can also empower workers across the entire organization. For example, Responsible AI can help ensure that AI systems schedule workers in ways that balance employee and company objectives. By building more sustainable schedules, companies will see employee turnover fall, reducing the costs of hiring and training – over $80 billion annually in the US alone.

Putting Principles into Practice

Despite the upsides of pursuing Responsible AI, many companies lack clarity about how to capture these benefits in their day-to-day business. The approach

---

7 https://www.bcg.com/featured-insights/how-to/purpose-driven-business.aspx.
8 https://www.bcg.com/publications/2017/total-societal-impact-new-lens-strategy.
9 https://www.bcg.com/publications/2019/decoding-digital-talent.
10 https://www.doteveryone.org.uk/wp-content/uploads/2019/04/PeoplePowerTech_Doteveryone_May2019.pdf.

many organizations take has been to create and publicize AI principles. In a comprehensive search of the literature, we found more than 80 sets of such principles. But nearly all lack information about how to make them operational. We consistently observe the gap between principles and practice – the Responsible AI Gap.

Principles without action are hollow. Lack of action not only fails to realize the upside potential of AI but could also be perceived negatively by customers and employees. To cross the Responsible AI Gap, direction is urgently needed. In fact, the practitioners building AI systems are struggling to take tangible action and asking for guidance: 78% percent of tech workers[11] surveyed by Doteveryone want practical methods and resources to help consider societal impact when building products (Figure 17.1).

Sources: Center for the Governance of AI, University of Oxford; Doteveryone; BCG research and analysis.

Figure 17.1: Responsible AI principles have not altered AI practices.

Overcoming these challenges requires going far beyond a narrow focus on the algorithms that power AI. Companies must look at every aspect of end-to-end AI systems. They must address front-end practices such as data collection, data processing, and data storage – and pay heed as well to back-end practices, including the business processes in which a system will be used, the decision makers who will determine when and where to implement a system, and the ways information will be presented. They must also ensure that the systems are robust, while keeping top of mind all the potential ways they can fail. They

---

11 https://www.doteveryone.org.uk/report/workersview/.

must also address the large-scale transformation and associated change management[12] that can generate the greatest impact.

From our engagements with multiple organizations, we have uncovered six basic steps to make Responsible AI real. While they may appear extensive, leaders should remember that they do not require a massive investment to get started. Each step can begin small and evolve and expand over time as an initiative matures. The important thing is that organizations should make progress across each of these steps (Figure 17.2).

Empower Responsible AI leadership
Appoint a leader and a diverse team to design and lead the Responsible AI program and drive initiatives.

Develop principles, policies, and training
Build, communicate, and disseminate Responsible AI principles, policies, and training to all members of the AI team, including leaders.

Establish human + AI governance
Establish roles and responsibilities, a mechanism for review and adherence, escalation paths to raise concerns, and accountability for outcomes.

Conduct Responsible AI reviews
Build or adopt a tool for conducting end-to-end use case reviews and ensure they are conducted at scale.

Integrate tools and methods
Evolve standard data, technology, and model building to include Responsible AI considerations.

Build and test a response plan
Create the roles and responsibilities, processes, and procedures to respond when a Responsible AI lapse occurs, as well as to periodically test and refine.

Source: BCG RAI.

Figure 17.2: Six Steps to Make Responsible AI Real.

1. **Empower Responsible AI leadership.** An internal champion such as a chief AI ethics officer should be appointed to sit at the helm of the Responsible AI initiative. That leader convenes stakeholders, identifies champions across the organization, and establishes principles and policies that guide the creation of AI systems. But leadership with ultimate decision-making responsibility is not enough. No single person has all the answers to these complex issues. Organizational ownership that incorporates a diverse set of perspectives must be in place to deliver meaningful impact.

A powerful approach to ensuring diverse perspectives is a multidisciplinary Responsible AI committee that helps steer the overall program and resolves complex ethical issues such as bias and unintended consequences. The committee should include representation from a diversity of business functions (for example, business units (BUs), public relations, legal, compliance, AI team), regions, and backgrounds. A recent BCG study[13] suggests that increasing the diversity of leadership teams leads to more and better innovation and improved financial

---

12 https://www.bcg.com/publications/2019/how-to-win-with-artificial-intelligence-ai.
13 https://www.bcg.com/publications/2018/how-diverse-leadership-teams-boost-innovation.

performance. The same is true for Responsible AI. Navigating the complex issues that will inevitably arise as companies deploy AI systems requires the same type of diverse leadership.

2. **Develop principles, policies, and training.** Although principles are not enough to achieve Responsible AI, they are critically important, since they serve as the basis for the broader program that follows. Responsible AI principles should flow directly from the company's overall purpose and values to provide clear links to corporate culture and commitment (Figure 17.3). Time must be invested to develop, socialize, and disseminate Responsible AI principles. The process of soliciting broad feedback from across the organization has the added benefit of identifying employee concerns and areas of particularly high risk. Ensuring that principles are communicated broadly provides employees with the context for initiatives that will follow.

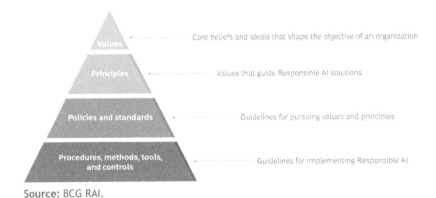

Source: BCG RAI.

Figure 17.3: Responsible AI Principles Should Flow Directly from the Company's Overall Purpose and Values.

A press release or companywide email is not enough to make principles real. Principles must be broken down into specific and actionable policies and standards around which teams can execute. Without these details, companies may fail to translate principles into tangible actions.

Ethical practices require systematic communications and training to educate teams about Responsible AI and a company's specific approach. Training needs to go beyond AI system developers to span all levels and areas of the business – from the C-suite to the end users of AI systems. Ultimately, Responsible AI is a shared commitment. Everyone has a role to play. Organizations need to foster an open "see something, say something" culture so that issues are identified and raised and that honest dialogue occurs around these complex and often sensitive matters.

3. **Establish human + AI governance.** Beyond executive leadership and a broadly understood ethical framework, roles, responsibilities, and procedures are also necessary to ensure that organizations embed Responsible AI into the products and services they develop. Effective governance involves bridging the gap between the teams building AI products and the leaders and governance committee providing oversight, so that high-level principles and policies can be applied in practice.

Responsible AI governance can take a variety of forms. Elements include defined escalation paths when risks emerge at a particular project stage, standardized code reviews, ombudspersons charged with assessing individual concerns, and continuous improvement to strengthen capabilities and confront new challenges.

4. **Conduct Responsible AI reviews.** For Responsible AI to have an impact, the approach must be integrated into the full value chain. Effective integration hinges on regularly assessing the risks and biases associated with the outcomes of each use case. Using a structured assessment tool helps identify and mitigate risks throughout the project life cycle, from prototype to deployment and use at scale. By assessing development and deployment at every step of the journey, AI practitioners can identify risks early and flag them for input from managers, experts, and the Responsible AI governance committee. These reviews should not be limited to the algorithms but be a comprehensive assessment of the complete, end-to-end AI system, from data collection to users acting on the recommendations of systems.

For example, a company might develop a recruiting model that prioritizes candidates for interviews based on their likelihood of receiving job offers. However, after using the assessment tool, the organization might realize that training the model on historical data from job applications is biased due to an underrepresentation of minority groups. Through a combination of data preparation, model tuning, and training for recruiters, the AI system could help increase the diversity of the candidate pool. Or consider an assessment of an e-commerce personalization engine that uses past purchase behavior and credit history to recommend products on a luxury retail website. The assessment tool could help the team identify that the engine systematically promotes products to lower-income individuals. A broader discussion could be triggered about the potential unintended consequences of a system that encourages purchases that might worsen the financial situation of some customers.

5. **Integrate tools and methods.** For Responsible AI principles and policies to have an impact, AI system developers must be armed with tools and methods that support them. For example, it is easy for executive leaders to require teams to review data for bias, but conducting those reviews can be time-consuming and complex. Providing tools that simplify workflows while operationalizing Responsible AI policies ensures compliance and avoids resistance from teams that may already be overloaded or operating under tight deadlines.

Toolkits comprising tutorials, modular code samples, and standardized approaches for addressing common issues such as data bias and biased outcomes are important resources. These learning resources should be made available to everyone involved with AI projects so that they can be applied to different contexts and guide individuals designing AI systems. Companies cannot require technical teams to address nuanced ethical issues without providing them with the tools and training necessary to do so.

Creating these resources may sound like a substantial undertaking. While that may have been true a few years ago, a variety of commercial and open-source tools and tutorials are now available. Instead of building their own resources, companies can begin by curating a set of resources that are most applicable to the AI systems they develop. Over time, resources can be customized to a company's specific needs in ways that limit a large up-front investment.

6. **Build and test a response plan.** Preparation is critical to making Responsible AI operational. While every effort should be taken to avoid a lapse, companies also need to adopt the mindset that mistakes will happen. A response plan must be put in place to mitigate adverse impacts to customers and the company if an AI-related lapse occurs. The plan details the steps that should be taken to prevent further harm, correct technical issues, and communicate to customers and employees what happened and what is being done. The plan should also designate the individuals responsible for each step, so as to avoid confusion and ensure seamless execution.

Procedures need to be developed, validated, tested, and refined to ensure that if an AI system fails, harmful consequences are minimized to the greatest extent possible. A tabletop exercise that simulates an AI lapse is one of the best tools companies can use to pressure-test their response plan and practice its execution. This immersive experience allows executives to understand how prepared the organization is and where gaps exist. It's an approach that has proven effective for cybersecurity[14] and can be equally valuable for Responsible AI.

---

14 https://www.bcg.com/capabilities/digital-technology-data/cybersecurity.

An Opportunity for Growth

While our approach may sound demanding, we firmly believe that delivering AI responsibly is achievable for any organization. Each step does not in itself require a massive initiative or investment. Companies can start with a small effort that builds over time.

The specific approach to the six steps we have described will differ depending on each organization's individual context, including its business challenges, organizational culture, values, and legal environment. Nevertheless, the fundamentals remain the same. Ethical leadership is critical, as is the establishment of broad-based support for the required internal change.

Fortunately, putting Responsible AI into practice does not mean missing out on the business value AI can generate. This is not an "either/or" issue, but rather a "both/and" opportunity in which Responsible AI can be realized while still meeting – and exceeding – business objectives. But for AI to achieve a meaningful and transformational impact on the business, it must be grounded in an organization's distinctive purpose. Only in that way can an organization build the transparency and trust that binds company and customer, manager and team, and citizen and society.

List of Figures

https://doi.org/10.1515/9783110775112-018

Index

https://doi.org/10.1515/9783110775112-019

CPSIA information can be obtained
at www.ICGtesting.com
Printed in the USA
JSHW011933240822
29712JS00002B/25